Italian Cooking for a Healthy Heart

Italian Cooking for a Healthy Heart

LOW-FAT, LOW-CHOLESTEROL GOURMET DISHES

Joanne D'Agostino, R.N., B.S.N., M.Ed.

IN COLLABORATION WITH

Frank J. D'Agostino, M.D.

A Lou Reda Book

EAGLE PUBLISHING CORP.
NEW YORK   1989

DEDICATED WITH LOVE
TO
Frank and Erica

Library of Congress Catalog Card Number: 89-084084
ISBN: 0-931933-79-X

Printed in the United States of America

10 9 8 7 6 5 4

Contents

Acknowledgments

Turning a concept into a reality is seldom the result of one individual's efforts. I hereby declare my indebtedness as follows:

My thanks, first and always, to God, upon whom I rely constantly for guidance and direction.

My love and deep appreciation to my husband, Frank, and daughter, Erica, whose patience, support, and tolerance during some of my failed culinary attempts gave me the incentive to keep trying.

To my mother, Pearl Minotti, whose life on this earth was full but all too brief, my eternal gratitude for daily lessons on life and the value of perseverance.

To my father, Carl Minotti, a special thanks for sharing with me his expertise in the art of Italian cooking.

To my sister, Marie Calandra, and cousin, Josie Regina, who shared my vision and my enthusiasm for this project and responded with encouragement and friendship, my sincere appreciation.

To all my family and friends who tested these recipes and offered helpful suggestions, a million thanks.

And finally, to my cousin and friend, Natalie Onorata, who is always there for everyone, a very special and sincere note of appreciation for the many hours spent assisting with the editing and preparation of the original manuscript.

Introduction

There is an old adage that says necessity is the mother of invention. This collection of recipes, born from the need to alter my methods of food preparation to accommodate my husband's health, is an example of the validity of that familiar statement.

In November 1986, Frank underwent angioplasty, a procedure he needed because of obstructed coronary arteries. He was discharged from the hospital with instructions from his physician to remain on a low-fat diet. Considering that he was fortunate enough to have escaped the need for coronary bypass surgery, a low-fat diet seemed a small price to pay. However, we knew that the task before us was not as simple as it appeared. Over the years we had made many unsuccessful attempts to adhere to various low-fat dietary regimens in an effort to lower Frank's serum cholesterol level. It was always a struggle to maintain such a diet for very long. Accustomed to eating the savory delectables of our Italian ancestry, we quickly became bored with the bland, lackluster foods usually included in low-fat diets. Moreover, none of the regimens we tried were restrictive enough to adequately effect a positive change in Frank's cholesterol level.

I knew that if we were to be "condemned" to a low-fat diet indefinitely, it would have to be one that we could live with *and* one that would produce the needed results. Having some background in medicine and nutrition (Frank is a physician and I am a nurse) aided us in formulating a plan of action. If the usual low-fat diet didn't work for us, we would have to devise a lower-than-low-fat diet! Thus, the impetus for this collection of recipes.

I have always risen to the occasion when faced with a challenge, but never before had the need to succeed been more imperative. Frightened and somewhat frustrated, I embarked on my new mission. I began by spending endless hours in the supermarket, reading food labels for fat and cholesterol content and recording the data. My evenings were spent reading and researching diet plans and food value manuals in an effort to determine the content and values of various foods. For months I survived on four hours' sleep each night and began each new day waiting in front of the supermarket for the doors to open at 8 A.M.

In the beginning, I was fooled numerous times by product labels. Frequently, I would grab an item from the shelf because it boldly boasted "no cholesterol," only to discover that it was high in fat content and contained hydrogenated oils and other ingredients not suitable for fat-restricted diets. Since the lowering of fats, in general, is an important aspect of the dietary program for individuals with coronary artery disease, it became apparent that I couldn't rely solely on "no cholesterol" labels.

My mission changed: I decided to compile a list of the low-fat or fat-free items in each food group (fruits, vegetables, dairy products, starches, etc.). Then, using only those products, I would attempt to duplicate, in a low-fat or fat-free manner, the old Italian recipes that our tastebuds were patiently and eagerly awaiting.

My kitchen became my laboratory, where I spent a good part of each day creating meals, measuring, recording, testing, tasting, and often discarding my failures. Approximately half of my recipes passed the taste test. The critics—my family—recommended a decent burial for those that didn't quite measure up. Admittedly, it was quite frustrating and demoralizing when an entire day's effort ended up in the garbage disposal, but in the end the successes put the failures far from mind.

The biggest reward came when I learned that my efforts had not been in vain. Frank's cholesterol level dropped 100 milligrams in a three-week period. Our new way of eating seemed effective, and the bonus payoff was that the meals tasted much the same as those we had always enjoyed. The lasagna, pizza, and cheesecake had returned. The only thing missing was the fat!

We had previously followed the guidelines offered by nutritional experts, which recommended that daily fat intake not exceed 30 percent of total calories and that cholesterol intake be restricted to under 300 milligrams daily. Frank's failure to respond to these levels made it apparent that they were still somewhat excessive for his needs. However, my new way of preparing foods enabled me to reduce our daily intake of fat and cholesterol by one half. To replace the lost fat calories, we increased our intake of complex carbohydrates, such as pastas, rice, and grain products, and ate ample helpings of fresh fruits and vegetables. All, of course, were prepared the low-fat way.

I suspect that, at this moment, there are many frustrated individuals struggling with the reality of having to lower their daily fat consumption. Some, perhaps, will take the time and initiative to scan the supermarket shelves, read the labels, do the research, and experiment, as I have done. Those individuals may have no need to read further. Others, however, may be willing to accept the fact that I have done the homework for them. It is for the latter group that these recipes are intended.

Medical Commentary

This book will serve no purpose if you are not convinced of the relationship between cholesterol and atherosclerotic coronary artery disease.

Blood cholesterol represents only one of several risk factors to one's cardiovascular health. Its importance, however, has surfaced more prominently than other factors over the past ten years, largely because extensive research conducted at top institutions worldwide has demonstrated a clear link between cholesterol levels and cardiovascular health.

We are now aware that until recently, what was considered a normal blood cholesterol level—115–295 mg/dl (milligrams per deciliter of blood)—was in fact too high. Indeed, average cholesterol levels of Americans undergoing "open-heart surgery" (coronary artery bypass grafting) were 220–230 mg/dl at several institutions in 1986. It is essential that we start in motion whatever it takes to reduce cholesterol levels below 200 mg/dl and keep them there.

If your physician concurs that lowering cholesterol is beneficial to your health, then dietary change should be the first step toward that end. From my experience, most people become confused when trying to decipher terms such as saturated fats, omega-6 and omega-3 polyunsaturated fats, hydrogenated products, high- and low-density lipoproteins and their ratios, triglycerides . . . All of these factors, however, have been taken into consideration in the preparation of these recipes. In fact, the recipes contained in this book have been created with stricter limitations on the amount of cholesterol, fats, and calories allowed than the recipes in most well-known and highly recommended heart diets. The evidence establishing the benefits of a diet like this one is now quite overwhelming.

My personal experience with this diet was dramatic: Within one month after my PTCA (percutaneous transluminal coronary angioplasty, or balloon procedure) for coronary artery disease, not only did my cholesterol drop precipitously (290 mg/dl to 191 mg/dl) but, in addition, so did my weight (140 pounds to 132 pounds). Not bad for one never considered more than a few pounds overweight. The explanation of course lies in the very low number of calories contained in these recipes, primarily because of their low fat content. One gram of fat provides 9 calories, as compared to one gram of protein or one gram of carbohydrate, each of which accounts for only 4 calories. These recipes, then, also benefit individuals with weight reduction in mind—a veritable bonus.

The problem of lowering blood cholesterol levels has become a national issue. The risk of atherosclerotic heart disease rises progressively with blood cholesterol levels above 200 mg/dl. A cholesterol-lowering diet is one way to curb this risk. Why not get a head start?

—*Frank J. D'Agostino, M.D.*

About This Book

This book is not intended as a complete dietary plan for a specific illness or condition. Individuals requiring such a regimen should consult their physicians. Furthermore, the author makes no recommendations as to the amount of fat or cholesterol or the number of calories one should consume in a day. This varies with each person and should be determined by his or her physician. Once a person's daily requirements are established, however, these recipes may prove helpful in maintaining that daily allowance.

Through the use of food value charts,* the number of calories per serving and the amount of fat and cholesterol per serving have been calculated and listed for each recipe. These values are intended as helpful guides for individuals who have been advised by their physicians to limit their daily intake of these items to specific amounts.

There are no magic ingredients in these recipes. In most cases, familiar foods are used in a way that eliminates unnecessary fats. Low-fat substitutes replace some standard ingredients.

You will note that the entrées in this book are prepared exclusively with poultry or fish because both contain less

---

*Jean A.T. Pennington and Helen Nichols Church, *Food Values of Portions Commonly Used*, 14th edition (New York: Harper and Row, 1985).

saturated fat than beef, lamb, pork, and most other meats. For those who desire a diet that is less restrictive in fats, veal or lean meats may be substituted in many recipes calling for chicken or turkey. Naturally, a substitution of this type would alter the food values listed with the recipe.

Special Ingredients Used in These Recipes

Egg Substitute—A nonfat, cholesterol-free egg product can usually be found in the frozen-food department of most supermarkets. If unavailable, you may substitute 2 egg whites for every egg required in a recipe.

Nonfat Butter Flavoring—A butter flavoring or extract that contains no fat may be used for this ingredient. Some supermarkets sell a powdered nonfat butter flavoring called Butter Buds, which can be reconstituted by adding water. It can generally be found on the shelves where extracts, flavorings, and spices are stocked.

Oil-Free Dressing—Oil-free salad dressings are available in both liquid and dehydrated forms and can be found on the shelves along with other prepared salad dressings.

Nonfat Bread and Crumbs—Pita bread has been used in many recipes in this book that require bread or breadcrumbs because it is usually made without oil, shortening, egg yolks, or milkfat. Other suitable breads may be available as well, but be sure to check the ingredients listed on the package. Breadcrumbs can be made easily by processing suitable nonfat bread in a blender or food processor. Products such as cracker meal or cornflake crumbs are also available in nonfat forms for use in most recipes requiring breadcrumbs.

Adapting Other Recipes to This Method

The recipes included in this book will serve as a foundation for your low-fat recipe collection. After working with them for a while, you will find that the possibilities of creating other new and exciting recipes are endless. Leaf through some of your old cookbooks and, using the recipes in this book as a guide, create your own variations by making the appropriate substitutions.

For example, when a recipe calls for sautéing in oil, substitute defatted chicken broth, wine, or even fruit juice for the oil. Use nonfat butter flavoring such as Butter Buds for recipes requiring the taste of butter. Dry-sauté whenever possible (that is, when your ingredients will produce their own moisture). Nonfat egg substitute or egg whites serve as an excellent low-cholesterol replacement for the real thing in many recipes that require eggs. Nonfat dairy products such as yogurt, skim milk, and cottage cheese can be used whenever their high-fat counterparts are called for. Sauces or soups processed with skim milk or nonfat yogurt are as excellent as those made with heavy cream.

You will be delighted with the endless variety of rich creamy salad dressings and vegetable toppings you can invent with nonfat yogurt, dry-cura cottage cheese, and spices. Try your hand at creating luscious desserts by placing some nonfat yogurt, fresh fruit, and gelatin in a food processor or blender

Use nonstick cooking or baking pans to eliminate the 10 to 12 grams of fat normally required to "lightly grease" a cooking utensil.

Substitute turkey or chicken in recipes calling for other types of meat. Make use of liquid smoke flavoring to duplicate the flavoring of smoked ham or bacon fat. Have that Sunday brunch of western omelet and pancakes you've been craving, but use egg substitute and turkey pastrami for the ham and eggs; and prepare your own pancake batter with whole-wheat flour, baking powder, egg substitute, and skim milk. Try making the pancakes on your nonstick griddle without greasing it. You'll be pleasantly surprised to find that they don't stick.

Choose the low-fat alternative whenever possible. The list of possibilities is virtually endless. Use your imagination!

APPETIZERS
AND
SNACKS

Melon with Pastrami Appetizer

    1   medium cantaloupe
    12   thin slices turkey pastrami (about 6 ounces)
    1   lemon
    3 or 4 small clusters green seedless grapes
           (optional)
           Freshly ground black pepper

Cut cantaloupe in half lengthwise, remove seeds, and slice into 12 wedges (6 from each half). Remove rind from each wedge and arrange wedges on large serving platter. Wrap or drape each wedge of melon with a slice of turkey pastrami. Cut lemon into 6 wedges and arrange around edge of platter. Garnish with clusters of green seedless grapes, if desired. Serve with a sprinkle of freshly ground black pepper.

SERVINGS: 6

PER SERVING
Calories: 54
Fat: 1.6 grams
Cholesterol: 29 milligrams

Monkfish Cocktail

1 pound monkfish
4 tablespoons tomato catsup
1 tablespoon prepared horseradish
1 tablespoon lemon juice
  Outer leaves of head of lettuce
4 lemon wedges

Cut monkfish into bite-size chunks and steam over boiling water until tender (about 15 minutes). Chill. Prepare cocktail sauce by combining catsup, horseradish, and lemon juice. Arrange monkfish on crisp beds of lettuce and serve as an appetizer with cocktail sauce and lemon wedges.

SERVINGS: 4

PER SERVING
Calories: 89
Fat: 0.9 gram
Cholesterol: 50 milligrams (estimated)

Raw Vegetable Antipasto with Dip

> 2 tablespoons dehydrated oil-free Italian salad dressing mix
> 1 cup low-fat sour cream (page 169)
> 2 cups broccoli flowerets
> 2 cups cauliflower flowerets
> 2 large carrots, cut into 2-inch sticks
> 2 stalks celery, cut into 2-inch sticks
> 1 cucumber, peeled and cut into ¼-inch slices

Combine dehydrated oil-free salad dressing mix with low-fat sour cream and blend thoroughly. Chill for 1 hour. Arrange vegetables and dip on large serving platter.

SERVINGS: 8

PER SERVING
Calories: 60
Fat: 0.5 gram
Cholesterol: 2 milligrams

Pita Pizza Snacks

4 small whole-wheat pita pockets
2 cups crushed tomatoes in purée
1 cup chopped onions
1 cup chopped green peppers
1 4-ounce can mushrooms, drained
1 teaspoon Italian seasoning*
  Salt and pepper to taste

Split open each pita pocket into 2 round halves and place on cookie sheet with inner side up. Spread tomatoes and remaining ingredients evenly over pitas. Bake at 350° until crisp (approximately 15 minutes). Serve hot.

SERVINGS: 8

PER SERVING
Calories: 64
Fat: 0.4 gram
Cholesterol: none

*Available in the spice section of most supermarkets.

Chickpea Nuts

    1   20-ounce can chickpeas (garbanzos)
    1   teaspoon salt
    ¼   teaspoon garlic powder
    ½   teaspoon onion powder

Drain chickpeas and spread evenly on nonstick cookie sheet. Mix together the seasonings. Sprinkle over the chickpeas. Bake at 350° for about 40 minutes, or until chickpeas are dried to a nutlike texture. Loosen with spatula occasionally while baking to prevent sticking. Allow "nuts" to cool thoroughly on cookie sheet before placing in serving bowl. Makes 2 cups.

SERVINGS: approximately 16

PER SERVING   (⅛ cup)
Calories: 31
Fat: 0.4 gram
Cholesterol: none

Eggplant Dip

1 medium eggplant
½ cup chopped onions
2 tablespoons chopped fresh parsley
1 tablespoon lemon juice
½ teaspoon salt
¼ teaspoon pepper
2 cloves garlic, minced
Cayenne pepper (optional)

Bake unskinned eggplant at 350° for 1 hour. Peel eggplant, mash it, then combine with remaining ingredients. Place in food processor or blender and purée. Chill. (For a spicier dip, add a small amount more cayenne pepper.) Serve with pieces of toasted pita bread. Makes about 1½ cups.

SERVINGS: approximately 24

PER SERVING (1 tablespoon)
Calories: 5
Fat: trace amount
Cholesterol: none

Onion Dip

 1 cup low-fat sour cream (page 169)
 2 tablespoons dried onion flakes
 ⅛ teaspoon garlic powder
 ½ teaspoon dried parsley flakes

Combine ingredients and chill. Serve as a dip with raw vegetables. Makes about 1 cup.

SERVINGS: approximately 16

PER SERVING   (1 tablespoon)
Calories: 10
Fat: 0.1 gram
Cholesterol: 1 milligram

Potato Chips

2 medium baking potatoes
½ teaspoon salt (or less)
½ teaspoon onion powder

Thinly slice well-scrubbed, unpeeled potatoes. Arrange in single layer on nonstick cookie sheet. Bake at 450° until crisp (approximately 40 minutes). Sprinkle with seasonings on both sides when potatoes are about half done.

SERVINGS: 4

PER SERVING
Calories: 50
Fat: 0.5 gram
Cholesterol: none

Roasted Chestnuts

2   dozen chestnuts

With a sharp knife, cut a slash through the shells of the chestnuts. Arrange them in a shallow baking pan and bake at 400° for about 30 minutes. Remove one, peel, and test for doneness. Chestnuts are cooked when shell is easily removed and texture is soft and mealy.

SERVINGS: 8

PER SERVING   (3 chestnuts)
Calories: 29
Fat: 0.2 gram
Cholesterol: none

SOUPS

Chicken Vegetable Soup

1   2- to 2½-pound stewing or frying chicken
2   cups sliced carrots
2   cups chopped onions
1½ cups chopped celery (stalk and leaves)
1   16-ounce can crushed tomatoes
    Salt and pepper to taste
2   cups cooked pasta (any of the smaller
        varieties, such as shells, elbows, bowties)

Place chicken in large soup pot and cover with water. Bring to a boil and skim off surface residue with a strainer. Purée carrots, onions, and celery in a food processor (or chop them finely) and add to pot, along with crushed tomatoes. Season with salt and pepper to taste. Cover and simmer for 2 to 2½ hours. Remove chicken, debone, shred, and return meat to soup. Refrigerate soup for several hours, preferably overnight, in order to allow excess fat to congeal on surface. Skim off fat, reheat, add cooked pasta, and serve.

SERVINGS: 6

PER SERVING
Calories: 194
Fat: 3.7 grams
Cholesterol: 46 milligrams

Split Pea Soup

1 1-pound package dried split peas
5 cups water
1 teaspoon salt
3 ounces turkey pastrami, minced

Rinse dried peas and place in soup pot with other ingredients. Bring to a boil. Reduce heat, cover, and simmer for 1½ to 2 hours, or until peas are cooked to a creamy consistency. Add more water if a thinner consistency is desired. One cup of cooked elbow macaroni may be added before serving, if desired.

SERVINGS: **6**

PER SERVING	(without macaroni)	(with macaroni)
Calories:	159	184
Fat:	1.6 grams	2.2 grams
Cholesterol:	11 milligrams	11 milligrams

Minestrone

         1 cup chopped onions
         1 clove garlic, minced
         1 stalk celery, diced coarsely
         ½ cup shredded cabbage
         2 medium carrots, diced coarsely
         2 medium potatoes, diced
         3 cups water
         1 8-ounce can peas (reserve juice)
         1 16-ounce can kidney beans (undrained)
         1 cup crushed tomatoes
         ½ cup chopped fresh parsley
           3 or 4 leaves fresh basil, minced
           Salt and pepper to taste
         1 cup cooked pasta (small shells or elbows),
           optional

Dry-sauté onions, garlic, celery, cabbage, and carrots in large soup kettle for 5 minutes. Add potatoes, water, and reserved juice from the canned peas, cover and simmer until vegetables are tender. Add undrained beans, tomatoes, parsley, and basil. Season to taste with salt and pepper. Cover and bring to a boil, then reduce heat and simmer for 30 minutes. Add peas and cook an additional 5 minutes. Serve as is or with a cup of cooked pasta added.

SERVINGS: 4

PER SERVING	(without pasta)	(with pasta)
Calories:	204	229
Fat:	1 gram	1.6 grams
Cholesterol:	none	none

Lentil Soup

1	1-pound package dried lentils
4	cups water
1	teaspoon salt
1	cup finely minced onions
¾	cup grated or finely chopped carrots
½	cup finely chopped celery
¼	cup rosé wine
1	tablespoon tomato paste
½	teaspoon garlic powder
	Black pepper to taste
⅛	teaspoon liquid smoke (optional)
1	teaspoon sugar (optional)

Rinse lentils and place in soup kettle with water and salt. Bring to a boil and skim off any debris that surfaces. Add remaining ingredients. Cover and simmer for 1 to 1½ hours, or until lentils are tender, stirring occasionally. Add more water if a thinner soup is desired.

SERVINGS: 6

PER SERVING
Calories: 243
Fat: 0.1 gram
Cholesterol: none

Cream of Potato Soup

2 cups diced potatoes
1 medium onion, puréed
3 tablespoons flour
3 cups skim milk
   Butter Buds equivalent to 3 tablespoons
      butter
1 teaspoon salt
   Salt and pepper to taste

In a large saucepan, cover diced potatoes with water and boil until tender (about 30 minutes). Drain and mash with fork or ricer; combine with puréed onion and mix until well blended. Set aside. In a small bowl mix flour with ¼ cup of the milk to form a paste. Gradually add a little more milk until mixture is the consistency of a thick white sauce. Pour white sauce into a soup kettle and stir over low heat until warm. Do not boil. Add Butter Buds, salt, and remaining milk. Continue cooking, stirring constantly, until mixture begins to thicken and bubble. Add mashed potato mixture and simmer for about 5 minutes longer. Season with additional salt and pepper, if desired.

SERVINGS: 4

PER SERVING
Calories: 160
Fat: 0.9 gram
Cholesterol: 3 milligrams

Cream of Broccoli Soup

2	cups chopped broccoli (flowerets and stalk)
2	cups defatted chicken broth
1	teaspoon chopped fresh parsley
¼	cup nonfat dry milk powder
½	teaspoon salt

In a large saucepan combine broccoli and chicken broth. Cover and cook until broccoli is tender (about 20 minutes). Remove from heat and cool. Add parsley, dry milk powder, and salt. Place in blender and purée. Reheat and serve.

SERVINGS: 4

PER SERVING
Calories: 60
Fat: 1 gram
Cholesterol: 2 milligrams

Tomato Soup

2 pounds canned plum tomatoes
6 scallions, minced
½ cup chopped fresh parsley
½ teaspoon oregano
¼ teaspoon salt
½ teaspoon sugar
1 tablespoon tomato paste
1 cup water

Combine tomatoes and scallions and purée in blender. Place in large saucepan and add remaining ingredients. Cover and bring to a boil. Reduce heat and simmer for 30 minutes. Serve with freshly ground black pepper.

SERVINGS: 4

PER SERVING
Calories: 63
Fat: 0.8 gram
Cholesterol: none

Cream of Cauliflower Soup

 2 cups chopped cauliflower
 ½ cup chopped onions
 2 cups skim milk
 ½ teaspoon salt (or to taste)
   Butter Buds equivalent to 2 tablespoons
     butter
   Chopped fresh parsley for garnish
   Freshly ground black pepper (optional)

Place cauliflower, onions, and milk in large saucepan and cook covered until tender (about 20 minutes). Cool slightly. Add salt and Butter Buds and purée in blender. Reheat. Sprinkle with fresh parsley and serve with freshly ground black pepper, if desired.

SERVINGS: 4

PER SERVING
Calories: 70
Fat: 0.6 gram
Cholesterol: 2 milligrams

Cream of Pea Soup

> 2 cups fresh peas
> ¼ teaspoon salt
> 1 cup water
> 1 cup defatted chicken broth
> 1 cup skim milk
>   Freshly ground black pepper

Combine peas, salt, and water in a medium saucepan; cover and cook until peas are tender. Cool. Place peas and liquid in blender and purée. Combine puréed peas with chicken broth and milk and heat, stirring constantly. Serve with freshly ground black pepper.

SERVINGS: 4

PER SERVING
Calories: 90
Fat: 0.8 gram
Cholesterol: 1 milligram

SALADS

Green Bean Salad

1 pound green beans
1 8-ounce can water chestnuts, sliced
½ cup sliced red onions
  Salt and pepper to taste
  Garlic powder to taste
1 tablespoon red wine vinegar

Wash green beans, snap off ends, and place in vegetable steamer. Steam until beans are tender but firm (about 12 minutes). Do not overcook. Cool. Combine with water chestnuts, onions, seasonings, and vinegar. Chill before serving, if desired.

SERVINGS: 4

PER SERVING
Calories: 49
Fat: 0.1 gram
Cholesterol: none

Orange Salad Roman Style

Outer leaves from large head of lettuce
4 medium oranges, peeled, seeded, and sliced crosswise
1 teaspoon oregano
⅛ teaspoon garlic powder
⅛ teaspoon salt
1 cup diced apples
1 tablespoon lemon juice
Few sprigs fresh parsley

Arrange bed of lettuce on bottom of large serving platter or on individual salad plates. Place orange slices on lettuce. Sprinkle with oregano, garlic powder, and salt. Combine apples and lemon juice and spoon over orange slices. Garnish with fresh parsley.

SERVINGS: 4

PER SERVING
Calories: 86
Fat: 0.4 gram
Cholesterol: none

Beet and Onion Salad

1 16-ounce can sliced red beets, drained
1 large onion, sliced and separated into rings
⅛ teaspoon garlic powder
⅛ teaspoon salt
¼ teaspoon oregano
  Coarsely ground black pepper to taste
1 tablespoon red wine vinegar

Combine all ingredients and toss. Chill before serving.

SERVINGS: 4

PER SERVING
Calories: 48
Fat: 0.1 gram
Cholesterol: none

Tomato, Onion, and Cucumber Salad

3   large ripe tomatoes
1   cucumber, peeled and cubed
½   cup chopped red onions
1   tablespoon minced fresh basil
    Salt and pepper to taste
⅛   teaspoon garlic powder (optional)
1   tablespoon red wine vinegar

Have all ingredients at room temperature. Cut tomatoes into bite-size wedges and place in salad bowl with cucumber, onions, and basil. Add salt and pepper to taste (and garlic powder if desired). Add vinegar and toss gently. This salad may be chilled, but the delicate flavor of the ripe tomatoes is enhanced when served at room temperature.

SERVINGS: 4

PER SERVING
Calories: 43
Fat: 0.4 gram
Cholesterol: none

Fresh Spinach and Mushroom Salad

2	lemons
1	cup sliced fresh mushrooms
1	pound fresh spinach
¼	teaspoon oregano
¼	teaspoon garlic powder
	Salt to taste

Squeeze the juice of 1 lemon over the mushrooms, stir, and set aside to marinate for a few minutes. Wash spinach and drain well. Cut spinach, place in salad bowl, and season with oregano, garlic powder, and salt. Add marinated mushrooms and juice to the spinach, tossing gently. Cut the second lemon into 4 wedges. Arrange spinach salad on individual salad plates and serve with lemon wedges.

SERVINGS: **4**

PER SERVING
Calories: 38
Fat: 0.3 gram
Cholesterol: none

Carrot Salad

6 carrots, grated or shaved
¼ cup orange juice
1 large orange, peeled, seeded, sectioned, and
chopped into small pieces
¼ cup dark raisins
Salt and pepper to taste
Outer leaves of head of lettuce
Fresh parsley sprigs (optional)

Combine grated carrots, orange juice, chopped orange, raisins, salt, and pepper; toss well. Line four salad plates with lettuce leaves. Spoon carrot salad onto lettuce bed. Garnish with sprigs of fresh parsley, if desired.

SERVINGS: 4

PER SERVING
Calories: 94
Fat: 0.4 gram
Cholesterol: none

Waldorf Salad

> 1½ cups chopped apples
> 1 cup chopped celery
> ½ cup dark raisins
> ½ teaspoon lemon juice
> ⅓ cup nonfat plain yogurt
> 1 teaspoon sugar
> Outer leaves of head of lettuce (optional)

In a medium bowl combine apples, celery, and raisins. Sprinkle with lemon juice and toss. Combine yogurt and sugar and add to apple mixture. Toss again until well blended. Serve on beds of lettuce on individual salad plates, if desired.

SERVINGS: 4

PER SERVING
Calories: 95
Fat: 0.5 gram
Cholesterol: 0.3 milligram

Tuna and Tomato Salad

1 6½-ounce can water-packed tuna, drained
8 cherry tomatoes, halved
3 scallions, chopped
1 tablespoon lemon juice
Outer leaves of head of lettuce (optional)

Combine tuna, tomatoes, and scallions in a medium salad bowl. Sprinkle with lemon juice and toss gently. Serve on beds of crisp lettuce, if desired.

SERVINGS: 4

PER SERVING
Calories: 76
Fat: 0.6 gram
Cholesterol: 29 milligrams

Zucchini and Onion Salad

   4 cups cubed zucchini
   1 cup chopped red onions
   1 tablespoon fresh chopped basil
   ¼ teaspoon garlic powder
     Salt and pepper to taste
   ½ cup low-fat sour cream (page 169)
     Outer leaves of head of lettuce

Steam chunks of zucchini for 3 minutes. Chill. Add onions, basil, garlic powder, salt, and pepper to zucchini Combine with low-fat sour cream and toss gently. Serve on crisp beds of lettuce.

SERVINGS: 4

PER SERVING
Calories: 66
Fat: 0.4 gram
Cholesterol: 2 milligrams

Three-Bean Salad

1 cup canned cut green beans, drained
1 cup canned chickpeas, drained
1 cup canned red kidney beans, drained
1 cup chopped red onions
1 cup chopped celery
1 teaspoon oregano
¼ teaspoon garlic powder
½ teaspoon salt (or to taste)
2 tablespoons red wine vinegar

In a large salad bowl combine all ingredients and toss well. Chill before serving.

SERVINGS: 6

PER SERVING
Calories·   96
Fat: 0.9 gram
Cholesterol: none

Chicken Salad Italiano

½	pound cooked chicken breast, cubed
1	large tomato, diced
1½	cups chopped iceberg lettuce
½	cup chopped onions
½	teaspoon salt
⅛	teaspoon garlic powder
⅛	teaspoon pepper
1	tablespoon red wine vinegar
1	teaspoon lemon juice
	Outer leaves of head of lettuce

Combine chicken, tomato, lettuce, and onions. Season with salt, garlic powder, and pepper. Sprinkle with red wine vinegar and lemon juice and toss well. Serve on crisp lettuce beds.

SERVINGS: 4

PER SERVING
Calories: 95
Fat: 1.3 grams
Cholesterol: 22 milligrams

Italian-Style Coleslaw

4 cups shredded cabbage
1 medium red onion, sliced and separated into
   rings
1 teaspoon Italian seasoning*
¼ teaspoon salt
1 tablespoon red wine vinegar

In a large salad bowl combine cabbage and onion. Season with Italian seasoning and salt. Add red wine vinegar and toss well. Serve chilled.

SERVINGS: 4

PER SERVING
Calories·   30
Fat·   0.2 gram
Cholesterol: none

*Available in the spice section of most supermarkets.

Creamy Cucumber and Onion Salad

	Outer leaves from head of lettuce
4	cucumbers, peeled and sliced
1	medium onion, sliced and separated into rings
¼	teaspoon salt
½	cup plain nonfat yogurt
1	teaspoon sugar
1	tablespoon red wine vinegar

Line four flat salad plates with beds of lettuce. Arrange cucumber slices and onion rings on lettuce. Season with salt. Combine yogurt, sugar, and vinegar, and blend thoroughly. Spoon dressing over cucumber salad. Serve chilled.

SERVINGS: 4

PER SERVING
Calories:	67
Fat:	0.4 gram
Cholesterol:	1 milligram

Green Bean and Water Chestnut Salad

1	pound fresh green beans
1	8-ounce can sliced water chestnuts
1	teaspoon Italian seasoning*
	Salt and pepper to taste
2	tablespoons lemon juice

Wash green beans, snap off ends, and steam until crisp but tender (about 12 minutes). Do not overcook. Cool. Add water chestnuts, Italian seasoning, salt and pepper, and lemon juice and toss well. Chill before serving.

SERVINGS: 4

PER SERVING
Calories: 45
Fat: 0.1 gram
Cholesterol: none

*Available in the spice section of most supermarkets.

Seafood Pasta Salad

  1 6½-ounce can water-packed tuna, drained
  ½ cup chopped red onions
  ¼ cup chopped celery
  1 cup cooked pasta (elbows or shells)
  1 tablespoon chopped fresh parsley
  2 tablespoons oil-free salad dressing
     Salt and pepper to taste

Combine tuna, onions, and celery and mix well. Add cooked pasta and fresh parsley and toss gently. Sprinkle with oil-free salad dressing and toss again. Season with salt and pepper to taste. Serve chilled.

SERVINGS: 4

PER SERVING
Calories: 101
Fat: 0.6 gram
Cholesterol: 28 milligrams

PASTAS

Spinach-Stuffed Shells

1 10-ounce package frozen spinach
¼ cup chopped scallions
12 ounces low-fat cottage cheese (1% or less)
Egg substitute equivalent to 1 egg
¼ cup skim milk (optional)
¼ cup chopped fresh parsley
½ teaspoon salt (or to taste)
¼ teaspoon pepper
¼ teaspoon garlic powder
20 large pasta shells
4 cups spaghetti sauce*

Cook spinach and scallions in small amount of water, following the instructions on the spinach box. Drain. Mix cottage cheese, egg substitute, milk (if necessary to thin), and parsley in medium bowl. Add spinach and onion mixture along with salt, pepper, and garlic powder. Mix thoroughly. Partially boil pasta shells (about 9 minutes) and stuff with spinach and cheese filling. Spread about 1 cup of spaghetti sauce on bottom of baking dish. Arrange shells in dish and top with remaining 3 cups of spaghetti sauce. Cover and bake at 350° for 30 minutes.

SERVINGS: 4

PER SERVING
Calories: 290

Fat: 1.9 grams
Cholesterol: 5 milligrams

*You can use the spaghetti sauce from the Spaghetti and Meatballs recipe (p. 56) or a plain meatless sauce. Do not use prepared bottled sauces that contain oils.

Pasta with Garbanzos

2 1-pound cans garbanzo beans (chickpeas)
1 cup chopped onions
½ teaspoon oregano
½ teaspoon garlic powder
  Salt and pepper to taste
1 14-ounce can stewed tomatoes, chopped
½ teaspoon sugar
¼ cup red wine (optional)
3 cups cooked elbow macaroni or small shells

Put garbanzo beans and their liquid in a large saucepan with onions, oregano, garlic powder, salt, and pepper. Cook over medium heat for 10 minutes. Add stewed tomatoes, sugar, and wine (if desired). Bring to a boil; cover, reduce heat, and simmer for 30 minutes. Add cooked pasta and stir well. Serve in soup bowls as a side dish.

SERVINGS: 6

PER SERVING
Calories: 242
Fat: 2.3 grams
Cholesterol: none

Baked Ziti Ragu

Tomato Sauce
  1 pound ground turkey
  ½ cup chopped onions
  ½ teaspoon salt
  ¼ teaspoon pepper
  ½ teaspoon oregano
  ¼ teaspoon garlic powder
  1 28-ounce can crushed tomatoes in purée
  1 6-ounce can tomato paste
  1 cup water
  1 teaspoon sugar

Macaroni and Cheese Mixture
  4 cups low-fat cottage cheese (1% or less)
     Egg substitute equivalent to 1 egg
  ¾ cup minced fresh parsley
  ½ teaspoon salt
     Dash of nutmeg (optional)
  ¼ teaspoon garlic powder (optional)
  1 pound ziti, parboiled (firm)

Crumble turkey meat in 4-quart nonstick sauce pot or Dutch oven. Add onions, salt, pepper, oregano, and garlic powder. Sauté until turkey is cooked, stirring frequently. Add crushed tomatoes, tomato paste, water, and sugar. Cover and simmer for 30 to 40 minutes.

While sauce is cooking, combine cottage cheese, egg substitute, parsley, salt, nutmeg, and garlic powder; mix thoroughly.

Spread 1 cup of tomato sauce in bottom of lasagna

pan. Combine parboiled ziti with cheese mixture and stir well. Spoon ziti and cheese into lasagna pan. Reserve 1 cup of tomato sauce and pour remaining sauce over ziti and cheese. Cover with aluminum foil and bake at 350° for 45 minutes. Top with reserved, heated tomato sauce when serving.

SERVINGS: 8

PER SERVING
Calories: 332
Fat: 3.2 grams
Cholesterol: 43 milligrams

Spaghetti with Cauliflower Sauce

1   head cauliflower
¾   cup water with ½ teaspoon salt added
1   cup chopped onions
2   tablespoons white wine
3   tablespoons white raisins
¼   teaspoon pepper
    Salt to taste
1   pound spaghetti, cooked
    Freshly ground black pepper

Wash cauliflower, cut and separate into flowerets, and place in saucepan with salted water. Cover and cook until tender (about 20 minutes). Drain cauliflower, reserving the liquid. Mash cauliflower. In a nonstick skillet, sauté onions with wine until tender. Add mashed cauliflower, raisins, pepper, and ¼ cup reserved cauliflower liquid. Season with additional salt to taste. Simmer for 10 to 15 minutes, stirring frequently. If cauliflower becomes too dry, add a little more reserved liquid or water. Serve over cooked spaghetti with freshly ground pepper.

SERVINGS: 6

PER SERVING
Calories: 241
Fat: 1.4 grams
Cholesterol: none

Beans and Pasta

1	1-pound package dried beans (pinto, northern, etc.)*
1	cup chopped onions
1	teaspoon salt
½	teaspoon garlic powder
1	28-ounce can crushed tomatoes
1	teaspoon sugar
½	teaspoon pepper
½	teaspoon oregano
½	pound spaghetti, broken into 2-inch pieces and cooked

Place beans in a large saucepan, cover with water, and cook until tender (approximately 1 hour). Add all other ingredients, except pasta, and cook for an additional 45 minutes. If necessary, add a little more water to obtain a soup-like consistency. Just before serving, add cooked spaghetti. Stir thoroughly and serve immediately in soup bowls, as a side dish.

SERVINGS: 6

PER SERVING
Calories: 285
Fat: 1.6 grams
Cholesterol: none

*Two 16-ounce cans of cannellini beans may be substituted for dried beans. If these precooked beans are used, you may eliminate the first step.

Spaghetti with Eggplant Sauce

1	1- to 1½-pound eggplant, peeled and cubed
½	cup chopped onions
2	tablespoons chopped fresh parsley
1	teaspoon salt
¼	teaspoon pepper
1	clove garlic, minced
1	4-ounce can mushrooms, undrained
½	pound ground turkey
1	teaspoon oregano
¼	cup red wine
1	28-ounce can crushed tomatoes in purée
1	6-ounce can tomato paste
1	cup water
1	teaspoon sugar
1½	pounds spaghetti, cooked

In a 4-quart nonstick sauce pot or Dutch oven, dry-sauté eggplant and onions together for 5 minutes. Add parsley, salt, pepper, garlic, and undrained mushrooms. Cover and simmer for 15 minutes, stirring occasionally. In a large nonstick skillet, sauté ground turkey, oregano, and wine. Simmer until turkey is cooked, stirring frequently. Add crushed tomatoes, tomato paste, water, and sugar. Mix thoroughly and add to eggplant. Stir well. Bring to a boil; reduce heat and simmer for about 40 minutes, stirring frequently. Serve over cooked spaghetti.

SERVINGS: 8

PER SERVING		Fat:	2.7 grams
Calories:	326	Cholesterol:	19 milligrams

Spaghetti with Bolognese-Style Ragu

½ cup chopped onions
½ cup chopped carrots
¼ cup chopped celery
1 pound ground turkey
½ teaspoon salt (or to taste)
¼ teaspoon pepper
1 28-ounce can crushed tomatoes
1 6-ounce can tomato paste
1 cup water
3 tablespoons evaporated skim milk
Butter Buds equivalent to 1 tablespoon butter
1 pound spaghetti, cooked

In a large nonstick skillet, dry-sauté onions, carrots, and celery until tender. Add crumbled ground turkey, salt, and pepper and cook until done, stirring frequently. Combine tomatoes, tomato paste, water, milk, and Butter Buds and add to turkey. Blend thoroughly. Cover and simmer for 45 minutes, stirring occasionally. Serve over cooked spaghetti.

SERVINGS: 6

PER SERVING
Calories: 358
Fat: 3.2 grams
Cholesterol: 44 milligrams

Linguine with Clam Sauce

3   6½-ounce cans minced clams with juice
¼   teaspoon garlic powder
1   28-ounce can crushed tomatoes
1   8-ounce can tomato sauce
1   6-ounce can tomato paste
1   cup water
¼   teaspoon salt
    Pepper to taste
1   teaspoon sugar
½   cup chopped fresh parsley
1   pound linguine, cooked

Place clams and juice in large saucepan with garlic powder. Bring to a boil and simmer for 3 to 4 minutes. Add all other ingredients, except parsley and linguine. Stir, cover, and simmer for 45 minutes. Add parsley and cook an additional 5 minutes. Serve over cooked linguine.

SERVINGS: 6

PER SERVING
Calories: 320
Fat: 2.8 grams
Cholesterol: 42 milligrams

Spaghetti with Fresh Mushroom Sauce

1½	pounds fresh mushrooms
½	cup chopped onions
2	cloves garlic, minced
2	tablespoons white wine
	Butter Buds equivalent to 2 tablespoons butter
	Salt and pepper to taste
1	28-ounce can chopped plum tomatoes
3	tablespoons tomato paste
½	cup water
½	cup chopped fresh parsley
1	pound spaghetti, cooked

Wash, dry, and slice mushrooms. Set aside. In a large nonstick skillet, sauté onions and garlic with wine and Butter Buds until onions are translucent. Add mushrooms, salt, and pepper. Cook over medium-high heat, stirring constantly, for 3 to 4 minutes. Reduce heat. Add tomatoes, tomato paste, and water; mix well. Cover and simmer for 40 minutes. Add parsley during last minute of cooking time. Serve over cooked spaghetti.

SERVINGS: 6

PER SERVING
Calories: 261
Fat: 1.8 grams
Cholesterol: none

Elbow Macaroni with Peas and Onions

1	cup chopped onions
1	tablespoon white wine
2	16-ounce cans peas with juice
1	8-ounce can tomato sauce
1	6-ounce can tomato paste
½	cup water
	Salt and pepper to taste
½	pound elbow macaroni, cooked

In a medium saucepan, sauté onions with wine. Drain peas, reserving juice. Combine tomato sauce, tomato paste, water, and reserved juice from peas. Add to saucepan containing onions and mix thoroughly. Bring to a boil, reduce heat, cover, and simmer for 15 to 20 minutes. Add peas and season with salt and pepper. Simmer for an additional 10 minutes. Combine with cooked elbow macaroni. Serve in small soup bowls as a side dish.

SERVINGS: 4

PER SERVING
Calories:	319
Fat:	1.7 grams
Cholesterol:	none

Lasagna

Tomato Sauce
- 1 pound ground turkey
- ½ cup chopped onions
- ½ teaspoon salt
- ¼ teaspoon pepper
- ¼ teaspoon garlic powder
- ½ teaspoon oregano
- 1 28-ounce can crushed tomatoes in purée
- 1 6-ounce can tomato paste
- 1 cup water

Cheese Filling
- 4 cups low-fat cottage cheese (1% or less)
- Egg substitute equivalent to 1 egg
- ¾ cup minced fresh parsley
- ½ teaspoon salt
- Dash of nutmeg

- 1 pound parboiled lasagna noodles (firm)

Crumble turkey in a 4-quart nonstick sauce pot or Dutch oven. Add onions, salt, pepper, garlic power, and oregano. Dry-sauté until onions are tender and turkey is thoroughly cooked. Add tomatoes, tomato paste, and water. Cover and simmer for 30 minutes. While sauce is simmering, combine cottage cheese, egg substitute, parsley, salt, and nutmeg in a large bowl. Mix thoroughly.

Beginning with a layer of tomato sauce, layer ingredients in the following order in a large lasagna pan:

noodles, cheese mixture, tomato sauce. Repeat layers, ending with a layer of noodles topped with tomato sauce. Cover with aluminum foil and bake at 350° for 1 hour. Remove from oven and let stand for 10 to 15 minutes before cutting and serving.

SERVINGS: 8

PER SERVING
Calories: 329
Fat: 2.7 grams
Cholesterol: 39 milligrams

Spaghetti and Meatballs

Tomato Sauce
- 2   cloves garlic, minced
- ¼   cup red wine
- 2   28-ounce cans crushed tomatoes in purée
- 1   12-ounce can tomato paste
- 1   8-ounce can tomato sauce
- 2   cups water
- ½   teaspoon oregano
- ½   teaspoon dried basil
- 1   teaspoon sugar (optional)
- ½   teaspoon salt (or to taste)
- ¼   teaspoon pepper

Meatballs
- 1   pound ground turkey
  Egg substitute equivalent to 1 egg
- 4   slices nonfat bread, soaked in water, with excess squeezed out
- 1   cup finely minced onions
- 2   cloves garlic, minced
- 2   tablespoons chopped fresh parsley
- 2   tablespoons chopped fresh basil
- 1   teaspoon salt
- ½   teaspoon pepper
        ketchup
- 1½ to 2   pounds pasta, cooked

To make the sauce, sauté garlic in wine. Add all other ingredients and mix thoroughly. Cover and bring to a boil; then reduce heat and simmer while preparing meatballs.

To make the meatballs, combine all ingredients in a large bowl and mix thoroughly. Form into balls approximately 2 inches in diameter. Place on cookie sheet and broil about 7 to 10 minutes, turning to brown on all sides. Remove from cookie sheet and drain on paper towels for several minutes. Add meatballs to tomato sauce. Cover and simmer for 1½ to 2 hours, stirring occasionally. Serve over your favorite cooked pasta.

SERVINGS: 8–10
PER SERVING   (1⅓ cups cooked pasta and 2 meatballs)
Calories: 354
Fat: 2.7 grams
Cholesterol: 37 milligrams

Seafood Spaghetti Sauce

2	pounds bluefish or haddock
¼	cup red wine
½	teaspoon oregano
½	teaspoon dried basil
2	tablespoons chopped fresh parsley
1	clove garlic, minced
½	teaspoon salt
¼	teaspoon black pepper
1	28-ounce can crushed tomatoes
1	28-ounce can tomato purée
1	teaspoon sugar (optional)

1½ to 2   pounds spaghetti, cooked

Poach fish fillets with wine, herbs, and seasonings in large, uncovered deep skillet or Dutch oven for about 15 minutes. Add crushed tomatoes, tomato purée, and sugar. Cover and bring to a boil. Reduce heat and simmer for 1 to 1½ hours, stirring occasionally. Serve fish and sauce over cooked spaghetti.

SERVINGS: 8–10

PER SERVING	(1⅓ cups cooked pasta)
Calories	371
Fat	3.7 grams
Cholesterol	50 milligrams

Pasta with Chicken Sauce

1	pound boneless chicken breast
1	cup chopped onions
1	tablespoon white wine
¼	teaspoon salt
⅛	teaspoon pepper
¼	teaspoon garlic powder
½	teaspoon oregano
1	28-ounce can crushed tomatoes in purée
1	6-ounce can tomato paste
1	cup water
1	teaspoon sugar (optional)
2	tablespoons chopped fresh parsley
1	pound spaghetti, cooked

Cut chicken into 1½-inch chunks. In a 4-quart Dutch oven or sauce pot, sauté onions with wine for 2 minutes. Add chicken, salt, pepper, garlic powder, and oregano. Continue cooking until onions are tender and chicken is lightly browned. Add tomatoes, tomato paste, and water; blend thoroughly. Cover and simmer for 1½ to 2 hours, stirring occasionally. Taste and add sugar if desired. Stir in fresh parsley during last 5 minutes of cooking time. Serve sauce over cooked spaghetti.

SERVINGS: 6

PER SERVING
Calories: 352
Fat: 3.6 grams
Cholesterol: 44 milligrams

Pasta with Shark Sauce

½ cup chopped onions
1 tablespoon dry white wine
1 pound shark steak
1 28-ounce can crushed tomatoes
1 6-ounce can tomato paste
1 cup water
½ teaspoon oregano
½ teaspoon salt
½ pound spaghetti, cooked

In a large nonstick frying pan or Dutch oven, sauté onions in wine. Add shark steak and cook uncovered for 5 minutes on each side. Combine tomatoes, tomato paste, water, oregano, and salt. Blend well, then add to shark steak. Cover and simmer for 1 to 1½ hours, stirring occasionally. Carefully remove fish from sauce. Serve sauce over cooked spaghetti as a side dish with the fish.

SERVINGS: 4

PER SERVING
Calories: 386
Fat: 4 grams
Cholesterol: 62 milligrams

VEGETABLES

Baked Stuffed Acorn Squash

    1 large acorn squash (4 to 5 inches in diameter)
       Butter Buds equivalent to 2 teaspoons butter
    1 teaspoon brown sugar
    6 tablespoons applesauce
       Cinnamon to taste

Cut acorn squash in half lengthwise and remove seeds. Place halves skin side up on baking dish and bake at 400° for 40 minutes, or until squash can be easily pierced with a pointed knife. Remove from oven and cool slightly. Invert squash and scoop out pulp, leaving shell with just enough squash to retain shape (about ¼ inch). Mash pulp and add Butter Buds, brown sugar, and applesauce. Mix well. Refill shells with mixture and sprinkle with cinnamon. Place filled shells back in oven until thoroughly heated.

Variation: Substitute 6 tablespoons crushed pineapple in juice for the applesauce and brown sugar.

SERVINGS: 2

PER SERVING
Calories: 80
Fat: 0.1 gram
Cholesterol: none

Broccoli Italiano

1	large bunch broccoli (about 1½ pounds)
¼	cup water
½	teaspoon garlic powder
¼	teaspoon crushed red pepper
	Salt to taste

Wash and drain broccoli. Remove tough outer skin of stalk. Chop flowerets and tender portions of stalk into bite-size chunks. In a large nonstick skillet, heat water to a boil. Add broccoli, garlic powder, and red pepper. Cover and cook on low heat for about 10 minutes, or until broccoli is tender and most of the water has evaporated. Stir occasionally. If broccoli becomes too dry before it is sufficiently cooked, add a little more water. Season with salt to taste.

SERVINGS: 4

PER SERVING
Calories: 40
Fat: 0.4 gram
Cholesterol: none

Stuffed Mushrooms

12 large mushrooms (1½-inch diameter)
1 cup minced onions
¼ teaspoon garlic powder
¼ teaspoon oregano
¼ teaspoon salt
Butter Buds equivalent to 2 tablespoons butter
1 tablespoon chopped fresh parsley
¾ cup toasted breadcrumbs from nonfat bread

Wash and drain mushrooms. Remove stems and set caps aside. Finely chop stems and dry-sauté with onions, garlic powder, oregano, and salt until onions are translucent. Add a few drops of water, if necessary, to prevent sticking. Add Butter Buds and parsley; stir well. Add toasted breadcrumbs and toss until crumbs are moistened. Fill mushroom caps with stuffing. Arrange on cookie sheet and bake at 400° for 30 minutes.

SERVINGS: 4

PER SERVING
Calories: 76
Fat: 0.5 gram
Cholesterol: none

Fried Cabbage and Apple Medley

1	medium head red cabbage, shredded
1	cup chopped onions
¾	teaspoon salt
¼	teaspoon pepper
4	tablespoons red wine vinegar
2	tablespoons water
1	tablespoon sugar
3	medium apples, peeled, cored, and diced

Place cabbage, onions, salt, and pepper in large non-stick skillet and dry-sauté until cabbage becomes limp. Combine vinegar, water, and sugar. Add to cabbage and mix thoroughly. Fold in apples, cover, and cook over low heat for 1 hour, or until cabbage is tender. Stir occasionally and add water, if necessary, to prevent sticking.

SERVINGS: 6

PER SERVING
Calories: 74
Fat: 0.5 gram
Cholesterol: none

Roasted Peppers

2 large green peppers
2 large red peppers
1 clove garlic, minced
½ teaspoon salt
½ cup finely chopped scallions
½ teaspoon oregano
3 tablespoons red wine vinegar
⅛ teaspoon crushed red pepper (optional)

Wash and dry peppers. Place in shallow pan and broil, turning peppers, until skin is evenly charbroiled on all sides (about 15 minutes). Immediately place peppers in pot and cover tightly with lid until peppers are cool. (The steam created in the closed pot will make removal of charbroiled skin easier.) When peppers are cool, remove charred skin. Cut peppers in half lengthwise and remove stems, seeds, and pulp. Slice peppers into lengthwise strips and place in bowl. Add remaining ingredients and mix well. Serve warm or chilled as a side dish with poultry or fish, or as an antipasto.

SERVINGS: 4

PER SERVING
Calories: 35
Fat: 0.2 gram
Cholesterol: none

Roasted Mushrooms

1	pound fresh mushrooms
1	teaspoon oregano
¼	teaspoon garlic powder
	Salt to taste
	Crushed red pepper to taste (optional)
1	tablespoon red wine vinegar

Wash and dry mushrooms. Place them stem up on a cookie sheet and roast in 400° oven for 20 to 25 minutes. Remove from oven, cool, and drain off any liquid that has accumulated. Cut mushrooms into halves or quarters. Add seasonings and wine vinegar and toss gently. Serve as a side dish with meat or fish, at room temperature or after reheating them for several minutes in a hot oven.

SERVINGS: 4

PER SERVING
Calories: 16
Fat: 0.1 gram
Cholesterol: none

Fried Cabbage with Tomatoes

1 medium head cabbage
1 large onion, sliced and separated into rings
¼ cup red wine
½ teaspoon garlic powder
1 teaspoon oregano
1 tablespoon chopped fresh parsley
  Salt to taste
  Crushed red pepper to taste (optional)
2 cups crushed tomatoes
1 tablespoon sugar

Cut cabbage into 1½- to 2-inch chunks. In a large nonstick skillet, stir-fry cabbage and onion with wine for about 10 minutes, or until cabbage begins to become limp. Season with garlic powder, oregano, parsley, salt, and red pepper (if desired). Combine tomatoes and sugar and add to cabbage, mixing thoroughly. Cover and simmer until cabbage is tender (about 30 minutes). Stir occasionally and, if necessary, add a small amount of water to prevent sticking.

SERVINGS: 8

PER SERVING
Calories: 38
Fat: 0.2 gram
Cholesterol: none

Snow Peas L'Arancio

         4   tablespoons orange juice
         1   pound snow peas
        20   seedless red or green grapes, halved

In a large nonstick skillet or a wok, heat 2 tablespoons
orange juice. Add snow peas and stir-fry until slightly
tender, but still crisp. Add the additional orange juice,
while continuing to stir-fry. Add seedless grapes; stir a
few more seconds and remove from heat.

SERVINGS: 4

PER SERVING
Calories: 51
Fat: 0.3 gram
Cholesterol: none

Glazed Cauliflower and Carrots

1   medium head cauliflower
2   medium carrots
½   cup orange juice
1   teaspoon finely minced fresh parsley

Wash cauliflower and separate into flowerets, cutting the larger ones into halves or quarters for uniformity of floweret size. Peel and julienne carrots. Heat half of the orange juice in a large nonstick skillet until it begins to boil. Add cauliflower and carrots and stir-fry over medium heat. Add the remaining orange juice a little at a time (it will evaporate during the stir-fry process) until the vegetables are glazed (about 10 minutes). Just before serving, sprinkle vegetables with minced parsley.

SERVINGS: 4

PER SERVING
Calories: 44
Fat: 0.2 gram
Cholesterol: none

Baked Zucchini and Eggplant

1   medium eggplant (about 1 pound)
1   teaspoon oregano
2   tablespoons chopped fresh parsley
1   teaspoon salt (or to taste)
¼   teaspoon garlic powder
⅛   teaspoon pepper
2   cups zucchini, peeled and cubed
2   medium onions, sliced and separated into rings
2   cups crushed tomatoes in purée

Wash unpeeled eggplant, cut into ½-inch-thick slices, and arrange in single layer in lasagna pan or similar baking pan. Sprinkle with about half of the herbs and seasonings. Next, spread cubed zucchini over eggplant slices and sprinkle zucchini with remaining herbs and seasonings. Arrange onion rings on top; then spoon crushed tomatoes evenly over all ingredients. Cover with aluminum foil and bake at 350° for about 40 minutes, or until eggplant is tender when pierced with a fork. Remove foil and bake for an additional 10 minutes.

SERVINGS: 6

PER SERVING
Calories: 54
Fat: 0.4 gram
Cholesterol: none

Stuffed Artichokes

4	fresh artichokes
½	cup chopped onions
2	cloves garlic, minced
2	tablespoons white wine
1	cup breadcrumbs from nonfat bread
1	teaspoon oregano
2	tablespoons minced fresh parsley
½	teaspoon salt
⅛	teaspoon pepper

Wash artichokes, remove stem and outer leaves, and cut off and discard approximately ½ inch of the tips of the leaves on the top of the artichoke. Set artichokes aside. In a nonstick skillet, sauté onions and garlic with wine. Remove from heat and add breadcrumbs and remaining seasonings. (Taste crumbs and adjust salt, if necessary.) Spread leaves of artichokes and stuff with breadcrumb mixture. Place artichokes in 6-quart pot with about 1 inch of water on the bottom. Cover and bring water to a boil. Reduce heat and simmer for 1 hour, or until a pointed knife can be inserted into the base of the artichoke with ease. Serve as an appetizer or as a side dish.

SERVINGS: 4

PER SERVING
Calories: 76
Fat: 0.2 gram
Cholesterol: none

Baked Cauliflower

1	medium head cauliflower
	Salt and pepper to taste
½	cup nonfat plain yogurt
3	scallions, minced

Separate cauliflower into flowerets. Place in pot or steamer with a small amount of water. Cover and cook until cauliflower can be pierced with a fork (about 15 minutes). Remove from heat and drain. Arrange cooked cauliflower in 9-inch-square ovenproof dish. Season with salt and pepper. Spoon yogurt over cauliflower and top with minced scallions. Bake uncovered at 350° for 25 minutes, or until lightly browned.

SERVINGS: 6

PER SERVING
Calories:	40
Fat:	0.3 gram
Cholesterol:	1 milligram

Eggplant Casserole

1   medium eggplant (about 1 pound)
    Salt and pepper to taste
2   cloves garlic, minced
1   teaspoon oregano
2   tablespoons chopped fresh parsley
6   ounces dry-curd cottage cheese
1   large onion, sliced and separated into rings
4   large ripe tomatoes, peeled and sliced
⅓   cup breadcrumbs from nonfat bread

Wash unpeeled eggplant and cut into ⅜-inch-thick slices. Season each slice with a small amount of salt. Stack slices in three or four piles on a large plate and set aside for about 1 hour. Then, pat each slice with paper towels to absorb moisture that has formed. Next, place a layer of eggplant on the bottom of a large lasagna (or similar) baking pan and alternate these layers: seasonings (garlic, oregano, parsley, and salt and pepper), cottage cheese, onion rings, tomatoes, eggplant. Repeat until all ingredients are used up. Top with breadcrumbs and additional salt and pepper, if desired. Cover with aluminum foil and bake at 375° for 45 minutes. Remove foil and bake 15 minutes longer.

SERVINGS: 4

PER SERVING
Calories: 96
Fat: 0.4 gram
Cholesterol: 2 milligrams

Mock Eggplant Parmesan

1	medium eggplant (about 1 pound)
3	tablespoons fine cracker crumbs or breadcrumbs (nonfat variety)
½	teaspoon salt
⅛	teaspoon pepper
½	teaspoon garlic powder
½	teaspoon oregano
1	cup chopped onions
2	cups crushed tomatoes
1	cup dry-curd cottage cheese

Peel eggplant and cut into ⅜-inch-thick slices. Combine crumbs, salt, pepper, garlic powder, and oregano. Press eggplant slices into crumb mixture, coating each slice thoroughly. Arrange slices on cookie sheet in single layer. Broil 6 to 7 minutes on each side to brown. While eggplant is broiling, dry-sauté onions until tender in medium nonstick saucepan. Add tomatoes; cover and simmer for 10 minutes. Place 2 or 3 tablespoons of tomato sauce on the bottom of a 9 × 13-inch baking dish. Arrange layer of eggplant slices on top of sauce. Place a small amount of cottage cheese on each eggplant slice; then top with additional sauce. Repeat layers until all ingredients are used up, ending with tomato sauce layer. Cover with aluminum foil and bake at 375° for 30 minutes.

SERVINGS: 6

PER SERVING		Fat:	0.4 gram
Calories:	90	Cholesterol:	2 milligrams

Mock Macaroni and Tomato Sauce

1 cup chopped onions
2 cloves garlic, minced
1 pound ground turkey
1 28-ounce can crushed tomatoes in purée
1 6-ounce can tomato paste
1 cup water
½ teaspoon salt
⅛ teaspoon pepper
1 teaspoon oregano
2 pounds fresh green beans
2 tablespoons chopped fresh parsley
Freshly ground black pepper

In a large nonstick skillet, dry-sauté onions and garlic until tender. (Add a few drops of water, if necessary, to prevent sticking.) Add ground turkey and cook on medium heat, stirring and crumbling turkey with a fork as it cooks. When turkey is done, add the next six ingredients. Cover and simmer for 40 minutes, stirring occasionally. While sauce is simmering, prepare green beans by removing ends and steaming 10 minutes, until crisp but tender. Do not overcook. Place cooked beans in large spaghetti bowl. Top with hot tomato sauce and sprinkle with fresh parsley. Serve with freshly ground black pepper.

SERVINGS: 6

PER SERVING
Calories: 156

Fat: 2.5 grams
Cholesterol: 50 milligrams

Sautéed Mushrooms

2	tablespoons white wine
2	cloves garlic, minced
1	pound fresh mushrooms
½	teaspoon salt
½	teaspoon oregano

Place wine and garlic in nonstick skillet and sauté. Add whole mushrooms and seasonings and cook uncovered about 12 minutes, or until all liquid evaporates, stirring frequently.

SERVINGS: 4

PER SERVING
Calories:	18
Fat:	0.1 gram
Cholesterol:	none

Oven-Fried Eggplant

½ cup nonfat cornflake crumbs
⅛ teaspoon garlic powder
½ teaspoon oregano
½ teaspoon salt
⅛ teaspoon pepper
1 large eggplant, peeled and cut into ½-inch-thick slices
Egg substitute equivalent to 1 egg

Combine cornflake crumbs with seasonings. Dip eggplant slices into egg substitute and then coat with seasoned crumbs. Arrange slices on nonstick cookie sheet and broil on both sides until brown (about 5 minutes per side). Serve as a vegetable side dish or sandwich filler.

Variation: Zucchini may be substituted for eggplant.

SERVINGS: 6

PER SERVING
Calories: 50
Fat: 0.4 gram
Cholesterol: none

Pepper and Onion Frittata

Egg substitute equivalent to 4 eggs
¼ teaspoon salt (or to taste)
Pepper to taste
½ cup chopped scallions or onions
½ cup sliced green peppers

Combine egg substitute with salt and pepper. In a 7-inch-diameter nonstick skillet, sauté scallions and peppers until tender. Distribute evenly over bottom of pan, then pour egg mixture over scallions and peppers. Tilt skillet as necessary to allow egg substitute to cover the entire surface of the skillet. Cover skillet and cook over low heat until frittata is almost firm (about 10 minutes). Remove from heat. With a spatula, carefully loosen frittata from edge of skillet. Cover skillet with an inverted plate with a diameter at least 2 inches larger than the skillet's. Holding plate firmly against skillet, carefully flip skillet, allowing frittata to be released onto plate. Next, slide frittata back into skillet, uncooked side down. Place skillet back on heat and continue cooking for a few minutes, until bottom side of frittata has firmed up. Remove from heat and slide onto serving platter. Cut into wedges for serving.

SERVINGS: **2**

PER SERVING
Calories: 73

Fat: 0.1 gram
Cholesterol: none

Broiled Tomatoes

2	large tomatoes, halved crosswise
2	tablespoons nonfat breadcrumbs
½	teaspoon oregano
¼	teaspoon salt
⅛	teaspoon garlic powder
1	teaspoon finely minced fresh parsley

Arrange tomato halves on pie plate. Combine remaining ingredients and sprinkle evenly over tomatoes. Place tomatoes under broiler for about 10 minutes, or until brown. Garnish with additional chopped parsley, if desired.

SERVINGS: 4

PER SERVING
Calories: 33
Fat: none
Cholesterol: none

Breaded Artichoke Hearts

1   14-ounce can artichoke hearts
    Egg substitute equivalent to 1 egg
½   cup nonfat cornflake crumbs
    Salt and pepper to taste

Drain artichoke hearts and cut into halves. Dip into egg substitute and press into cornflake crumbs, coating well on all sides. Arrange artichoke hearts on nonstick cookie sheet and heat under broiler until brown on all sides (about 15 minutes). Remove from broiler and season with salt and pepper to taste.

SERVINGS: 4

PER SERVING
Calories: 81
Fat: 0.9 gram
Cholesterol: none

POULTRY

Baked Chicken with Cheese and Tomato

¼	cup fine cracker crumbs or breadcrumbs (nonfat variety)
½	teaspoon salt
⅛	teaspoon pepper
½	teaspoon garlic powder
½	teaspoon oregano
1	pound chicken breast cutlets
1	cup chopped onions
1	cup crushed tomatoes
1	cup dry-curd cottage cheese

Combine crumbs, salt, pepper, garlic powder, and oregano. Coat chicken cutlets with crumb mixture and arrange on cookie sheet. Broil 3 to 4 minutes on each side to brown. (Broiling time may vary depending on thickness of cutlet.) Sauté onions in medium saucepan with a few drops of water until onions are tender. Add tomatoes, cover, and simmer for 10 minutes. Place 2 or 3 tablespoons of sauce on the bottom of a large baking dish. Arrange cutlets in a single layer over sauce. Top each cutlet with a small amount of cottage cheese, followed by tomato sauce. Cover with aluminum foil and bake at 375° for 30 minutes.

SERVINGS: 6

PER SERVING		Fat:	2.8 grams
Calories:	160	Cholesterol:	46 milligrams

Chicken Rollatini in Tomato Sauce

  1 pound chicken breast cutlets, thinly sliced
  2 medium onions, sliced and separated into rings
  3 ounces turkey pastrami, thinly sliced or shaved
  ¾ cup breadcrumbs from nonfat bread
  ½ cup chopped fresh parsley
  ½ teaspoon garlic powder
  1 teaspoon oregano
    Salt and pepper to taste
  ¼ cup red wine
  1 28-ounce can crushed tomatoes in purée

Lay chicken cutlets out side by side on flat surface. Distribute the following ingredients evenly on top of each cutlet: onion rings, pastrami, breadcrumbs, parsley, garlic powder, oregano, salt, and pepper. Roll each cutlet in jelly-roll fashion. Fasten with toothpicks or wrap with string, making certain that ends of cutlet are closed securely. Sauté chicken rolls in wine in large nonstick skillet for 15 minutes, turning on all sides. Add crushed tomatoes, cover, and simmer for 45 minutes, or until chicken is tender.

SERVINGS: 4

PER SERVING
Calories: 262
Fat: 5.5 grams
Cholesterol: 88 milligrams

Crisp Chicken Breasts

    1   pound boneless chicken breasts
    ½   cup oil-free Italian salad dressing
    1   cup cornflake crumbs
         Salt and pepper to taste
         Lemon wedges (optional)

Cut chicken into serving-size pieces. Marinate in salad dressing for about 1 hour, turning chicken once or twice. (Refrigerate while marinating.) Remove chicken from marinade and coat with cornflake crumbs, pressing chicken firmly into crumbs. Place chicken pieces on nonstick cookie sheet. Bake at 400° for about 35 minutes, or until chicken is lightly browned. Loosen chicken with spatula occasionally to prevent sticking, but do not turn chicken. Season to taste with salt and pepper. Serve with lemon wedges, if desired.

SERVINGS: 4

PER SERVING
Calories: 191
Fat: 3.9 grams
Cholesterol: 66 milligrams

Broiled Chicken L'Arancio

> 4 boneless chicken breast halves, skinned
>   (about 1 pound)
> 1 cup orange juice, freshly squeezed
> 1 tablespoon grated orange rind
> 1 teaspoon oregano
> ⅛ teaspoon garlic powder
>   Salt and pepper to taste
>   Orange wedges (optional)

Marinate chicken breasts in a mixture of orange juice, orange rind, oregano, and garlic powder for several hours. (Refrigerate while marinating.) Remove chicken from marinade and place on broiler rack. Broil about 7 minutes on each side, basting occasionally with marinade. Season with salt and pepper to taste. Serve with orange wedges, if desired.

SERVINGS: 4

PER SERVING
Calories: 180
Fat: 3.9 grams
Cholesterol: 66 milligrams

Crockpot Chicken Stew

                1   pound boneless chicken breasts
                2   tablespoons flour
                1   16-ounce can peas (drain and reserve liquid)
                2   tablespoons tomato paste
               ½   cup red wine
                3   carrots, thinly sliced
                4   medium potatoes, cut into 1-inch cubes
                1   teaspoon oregano
               ½   teaspoon salt
               ¼   teaspoon black pepper
               ¼   teaspoon garlic powder
                3   medium onions, chopped
               ½   cup chopped celery

Cut chicken into 1½-inch chunks and toss in a bowl with flour. Spread chicken pieces out on cookie sheet and place under broiler about 12 minutes to brown lightly on all sides; set aside. Combine reserved liquid from peas, tomato paste, and wine. Add a little water, if necessary, to bring total volume of liquid to 1½ cups; set aside. Place ingredients in crockpot in the following order: carrots, potatoes, chicken, dry seasonings, onions, and celery. Pour in liquid mixture and stir just enough to allow liquid to seep to bottom of crockpot. Cover and cook on low setting for 8 to 10 hours, or on high setting for 4 to 5 hours. (You may adjust cooking

time according to your crockpot instruction booklet.)
Add peas during last 15 minutes of cooking time.

SERVINGS: 6

PER SERVING
Calories: 198
Fat: 2.9 grams
Cholesterol: 44 milligrams

Chicken Scaloppine

      1 pound chicken breast cutlets, thinly sliced
      3 scallions, finely chopped
         Salt and pepper to taste
     ¼ teaspoon garlic powder
      1 teaspoon oregano
      1 tablespoon cornstarch
     ⅓ cup white wine
     ¼ cup tomato sauce
      1 teaspoon sugar
         Butter Buds equivalent to 1 tablespoon butter

In a large nonstick skillet, dry-sauté chicken cutlets with scallions. Add a small amount of water, if necessary, to prevent sticking. Season with salt, pepper, garlic powder, and oregano. Dissolve cornstarch in the wine and combine with tomato sauce, sugar, and Butter Buds, mixing well. Pour this mixture over cutlets. Cover and simmer for about 30 minutes. Thin the gravy with additional water, if necessary, during the cooking process.

SERVINGS: 4

PER SERVING
Calories: 186
Fat: ▼   3.9 grams
Cholesterol: 66 milligrams

Chicken Piccata

1	pound boneless chicken breasts, thinly sliced
¼	cup flour
½	teaspoon salt
¼	teaspoon pepper
	Butter Buds equivalent to 6 tablespoons butter
3	tablespoons lemon juice
½	cup white wine
2	tablespoons chopped fresh parsley

Coat chicken with flour and pan-fry quickly in large nonstick skillet, turning once. Season with salt and pepper. Combine Butter Buds, lemon juice, and white wine and add to skillet. Tilt skillet to distribute liquid evenly. Turn chicken once again, then cover and simmer until tender. Add a small amount of water, if necessary, to prevent juices from becoming too thick. Sprinkle with chopped parsley during the last minute of cooking time.

SERVINGS: 4

PER SERVING
Calories: 217
Fat: 3.8 grams
Cholesterol: 66 milligrams

Grilled Lemon Chicken Breasts

4 boneless chicken breast halves, skinned
Juice of 4 lemons
4 cloves garlic, minced
1 tablespoon oregano
2 tablespoons minced fresh parsley
½ teaspoon salt
3 tablespoons white wine
1 teaspoon grated lemon rind

Marinate chicken for several hours, or overnight, in a mixture of all above ingredients. Turn and baste several times while marinating. Cook chicken on barbecue grill or in broiler for 5 to 7 minutes on each side. Baste with marinade during cooking process.

SERVINGS: 4

PER SERVING
Calories: 177
Fat: 3.7 grams
Cholesterol: 66 milligrams

Chicken with Peppers

2 large green peppers, seeded and sliced into lengthwise strips
½ cup defatted chicken broth or bouillon
1 pound chicken breast cutlets, thinly sliced
½ teaspoon salt
¼ teaspoon pepper
¼ teaspoon garlic powder
½ cup white wine
1 teaspoon sugar
2 teaspoons cornstarch
2 teaspoons water

In a large nonstick skillet, sauté peppers in 1 or 2 tablespoons of chicken broth until peppers are slightly limp. Do not overcook. Remove peppers from skillet with a slotted spoon. Add chicken cutlets, salt, pepper, and garlic powder. Sauté for 1 to 2 minutes on each side. Add remaining chicken broth, wine, sugar, and peppers; mix well. Cover and simmer until chicken is tender. Mix cornstarch with water and add to skillet. Cook for several minutes more, until juice is thickened.

SERVINGS: 4

PER SERVING
Calories: 209
Fat: 3.9 grams
Cholesterol: 66 milligrams

Hunter's-Style Chicken Rosemary

     1   chicken, skinned and cut up (about 2
          pounds)
     ½   cup red wine
     1   cup chopped onions
     ½   teaspoon salt
     ¼   teaspoon pepper
     2   cloves garlic, minced
     2   teaspoons dried rosemary

Sauté chicken parts in 2 tablespoons of the wine for about 10 minutes, turning frequently. Add onions and seasonings and continue cooking until onions are tender. Add remaining wine. Cover and simmer for about 40 minutes, or until chicken is tender. Add a small amount of water, if necessary, to prevent sticking.

Variations: Add fresh or canned mushrooms with the onions, if desired, or add 1 teaspoon of tomato paste to the wine for a richer flavor.

SERVINGS: 4

PER SERVING
Calories: 194
Fat: 3.8 grams
Cholesterol: 66 milligrams

Chicken Cacciatore

9 Breast

1	pound boneless chicken breasts
1	cup chopped onions
2	cups sliced green peppers
1	4-ounce can sliced mushrooms
1	clove garlic, minced
1	teaspoon oregano
½	teaspoon salt
¼	teaspoon pepper
¼	cup dry red wine (optional)
1	28-ounce can crushed tomatoes in purée

Cut chicken into 1-inch cubes and pan-fry in large nonstick skillet for 5 to 7 minutes, stirring frequently to prevent sticking. Remove chicken from skillet. Place all other ingredients, except tomatoes, in skillet and sauté until onions and peppers are slightly limp. Add tomatoes and cook over medium heat for 5 minutes. Add chicken, reduce heat, and simmer for 45 minutes, or until chicken is tender.

SERVINGS: 4

PER SERVING
Calories: 230
Fat: 4.5 grams
Cholesterol: 66 milligrams

Roast Chicken with Herbs

2	pounds chicken parts, skinned
¼	cup red wine vinegar
¼	cup red wine
1	tablespoon dried rosemary
½	teaspoon oregano
½	teaspoon garlic powder
	Salt and pepper to taste

Arrange chicken parts in a shallow baking pan. Pour vinegar and wine over chicken and sprinkle with herbs and seasonings. Bake uncovered in 400° oven for about 45 minutes, basting and turning occasionally. Add a small amount of water if liquid evaporates before chicken is completely cooked.

SERVINGS: 4

PER SERVING
Calories:	180
Fat:	3.8 grams
Cholesterol:	66 milligrams

Turkey Sausage with Peppers and Onions

1	pound ground turkey
1	cup puréed onions
1	teaspoon fennel seed
1	teaspoon salt
½	teaspoon pepper
½	teaspoon liquid smoke
2	green peppers, seeded and sliced
1	large onion, sliced and separated into rings
	Salt and pepper to taste

Mix first six ingredients together and form into 4 patties. Broil on each side 5 to 7 minutes, until brown. Do not overcook. In a nonstick skillet, dry-sauté peppers and onion rings 3 to 5 minutes, until partially cooked. (Add a few drops of water, if necessary, to prevent sticking.) Season with salt and pepper to taste. Add cooked patties to skillet and smother with peppers and onion. Cover skillet and simmer until peppers and onion are tender, about 12 minutes. Serve as is or as a sandwich in pita bread pockets.

SERVINGS: 4

PER SERVING
Calories:	161
Fat:	3.1 grams
Cholesterol:	75 milligrams

Turkey Burgers

1	pound ground turkey
1	cup puréed onions
1	teaspoon prepared horseradish
1	teaspoon Worcestershire sauce
1	teaspoon salt
¼	teaspoon pepper
½	teaspoon garlic powder

Mix all ingredients together thoroughly and form into 4 patties. Broil on each side until brown (5 to 7 minutes) and drain off fat. Serve as is or in pita bread pockets with condiments (onion, relish, mustard, catsup) as desired.

SERVINGS: 4

PER SERVING
Calories: 155
Fat: 3.1 grams
Cholesterol: 75 milligrams

Turkey Meatloaf

❦

1	cup chopped onions
1	cup sliced carrots
1	pound ground turkey
3	slices nonfat bread or 2 small pita pockets
	Egg substitute equivalent to 1 egg
½	teaspoon salt
¼	teaspoon pepper
2	cloves garlic, finely minced
¼	cup chopped fresh parsley
1	cup tomato sauce
4	medium potatoes (optional)

Place onions and carrots in food processor and purée. Combine with turkey. Soak bread in small amount of water until well moistened. Squeeze out excess water and add wet bread to turkey. Add egg substitute, salt, pepper, garlic, and parsley. Mix thoroughly, using hands in a kneading fashion to ensure even distribution of all ingredients. Add 2 or 3 tablespoons of tomato sauce to the turkey mixture, if desired, for a softer meatloaf consistency. Form into loaf shape and place in roasting pan. Surround with quartered potatoes,* if desired; then pour remaining tomato sauce over meatloaf. Cover and bake at 350° for 1½ hours.

SERVINGS: 4

PER SERVING			
Calories:	214	Fat:	2.4 grams
		Cholesterol:	66 milligrams

*If potatoes are used, calories per serving will be 304.

Grease bottom of pan liberally

❦

Turkey Chili

1	pound ground turkey
1	cup chopped onions
2	medium green peppers, seeded and chopped
1	28-ounce can crushed tomatoes in purée
1	16-ounce can red kidney beans, drained
1	teaspoon salt
1	tablespoon chili powder
⅛	teaspoon dried basil

Place turkey, onions, and green peppers in large non-stick skillet. Cook over medium heat, stirring frequently to prevent sticking. When the ground turkey has faded from pink to white, add tomatoes, kidney beans, salt, chili powder, and basil. Stir well. Cover and simmer for 1 hour.

SERVINGS: 4

PER SERVING
Calories: 307
Fat: 3.9 grams
Cholesterol: 75 milligrams

Turkey Cutlets Italiano

1	pound turkey breast, thinly sliced
¼	cup red wine
1	cup chopped onions
1	4-ounce can mushrooms, drained
1	teaspoon oregano
2	cloves garlic, minced
½	teaspoon salt
¼	teaspoon pepper (crushed red pepper may be substituted for a zesty flavor)
1½	cups chopped plum tomatoes

Pan-fry turkey cutlets for 1 to 2 minutes on each side in a large nonstick skillet. Add wine and turn cutlets to coat on both sides. Add all other ingredients except tomatoes. Cover and cook over medium heat for 10 minutes, turning cutlets once or twice while cooking. Add tomatoes; cover and simmer for 1 hour, or until turkey is tender.

SERVINGS: 4

PER SERVING
Calories: 198
Fat: 2.4 grams
Cholesterol: 66 milligrams

Stuffed Turkey Bracciola

½ cup water
Butter Buds equivalent to 6 tablespoons
   butter
½ cup chopped onions
4 slices nonfat wheat bread, toasted and cubed
½ teaspoon oregano
¼ teaspoon garlic powder
½ teaspoon salt
Pepper to taste
¼ cup raisins
1 pound turkey breast, thinly sliced
2 tablespoons red wine
1 28-ounce can crushed tomatoes in purée
1 tablespoon minced fresh parsley

Boil water. Add Butter Buds and onions; simmer for 5 minutes. Add bread cubes and toss until water is absorbed. Season with oregano, garlic powder, salt, and pepper. Fold in raisins. Arrange cutlets on a flat surface and place a quarter of the stuffing in the center of each cutlet. Roll cutlet around stuffing in jelly-roll fashion and fasten with a toothpick. Sauté turkey rolls in wine in large nonstick skillet for 5 minutes, gently turning to coat with wine on all sides. Add tomatoes, cover, and simmer for 1 hour, or until tender. Sprinkle with minced parsley before serving.

SERVINGS: 4

PER SERVING		Fat:	2.5 grams
Calories:	278	Cholesterol:	66 milligrams

FISH

Baked Flounder

                1   pound flounder fillets
               ¼   cup chopped scallions
                1   teaspoon Worcestershire sauce
                    Butter Buds equivalent to 3 tablespoons
                       butter
               ¼   cup lemon juice
               ½   teaspoon salt
               ¼   teaspoon pepper
                3   tablespoons dry white wine
                1   lemon, sliced (optional)

Arrange fish fillets in shallow baking dish. Mix together remaining ingredients, except lemon, and sprinkle evenly over fillets. Top with lemon slices, if desired. Bake uncovered at 350° for 30 minutes, or until fish flakes.

SERVINGS: 4

PER SERVING
Calories: 140
Fat: 0.8 gram
Cholesterol: 56 milligrams

Baked Flounder Pizzaiola

1	pound flounder fillets
	Salt and pepper to taste
1	cup chopped green peppers
1	cup chopped onions
1½	cups crushed tomatoes in purée
	Butter Buds equivalent to 1 tablespoon butter
½	teaspoon sugar (optional)

Arrange fish fillets in single layer in shallow glass baking dish. Season with salt and pepper. In a nonstick skillet, dry-sauté peppers and onions for about 1 minute. Add remaining ingredients; mix well and pour over fish fillets. Bake uncovered at 350° for 30 to 35 minutes, or until fish flakes.

Variation: For a spicy touch, add 1 tablespoon red wine and a dash of crushed red pepper to the tomatoes.

SERVINGS: 4

PER SERVING
Calories: 135
Fat: 1.1 grams
Cholesterol: 56 milligrams

Flounder with Lemon and Clam Sauce

¼	cup lemon juice
1	pound flounder fillets
½	cup chopped onions
2	tablespoons white wine
1	cup minced clams in juice
¼	cup chopped fresh parsley
¼	teaspoon garlic powder
	Salt and pepper to taste
	Fresh parsley for garnish (optional)

Place 2 tablespoons of the lemon juice in the bottom of a large baking dish and arrange fillets on top. In a nonstick skillet, sauté onions and wine until onions are translucent. Add the next four ingredients and cook for 3 minutes. Spoon mixture over flounder and bake at 375° for 25 minutes. Garnish with additional chopped parsley before serving, if desired.

SERVINGS: 4

PER SERVING
Calories:	142
Fat:	1.4 grams
Cholesterol:	80 milligrams

Cod with Tomatoes and Raisins

½ cup chopped onions
2 tablespoons red wine
1 pound boneless cod
⅛ teaspoon garlic powder
Salt and pepper to taste
¼ cup chopped fresh parsley
1 cup chopped plum tomatoes
2 tablespoons tomato paste
4 tablespoons raisins

Sauté onions and wine in a large nonstick skillet until onions are translucent. Arrange cod in skillet on top of onions, and season with garlic powder, salt, pepper, and parsley. Cover and cook for 2 to 3 minutes. Combine tomatoes, tomato paste, and raisins. Spoon evenly over fish. Cover and continue cooking on low heat for about 15 minutes, or until fish flakes.

SERVINGS: 4

PER SERVING
Calories: 152
Fat: 1.1 grams
Cholesterol: 50 milligrams

Cod Véronique

         6 scallions, chopped
        ¼ cup white wine
         1 pound boneless cod
        ½ teaspoon salt
        ⅛ teaspoon pepper
        ¼ cup chopped fresh parsley
            Butter Buds equivalent to 2 tablespoons
                butter
        20 seedless red or white grapes, halved

Sauté scallions with half of the wine in a large nonstick skillet until they are tender. Arrange cod in skillet and season with salt, pepper, and parsley. Add remaining wine and Butter Buds. Cover skillet and cook over medium heat for about 15 minutes, or until fish flakes. Add grapes; cover and cook for an additional 2 minutes. Serve hot.

SERVINGS: 4

PER SERVING
Calories: 143
Fat: 1.2 grams
Cholesterol: 50 milligrams

Crabmeat Casserole

1	pound imitation crabmeat (usually a mixture of crabmeat and pollack or similar fish)
2	teaspoons lemon juice
1	teaspoon Worcestershire sauce
1½	cups skim milk
2	cups chopped cauliflower
½	teaspoon salt
⅛	teaspoon onion powder
½	teaspoon prepared mustard
	Butter Buds equivalent to 1 teaspoon butter
2	cups cooked brown rice

Sprinkle crabmeat with lemon juice and Worcestershire sauce; toss well. In a medium saucepan, combine milk and cauliflower and cook over medium heat until cauliflower is tender (about 15 minutes). Remove from heat and add salt, onion powder, mustard, and Butter Buds to cauliflower. Place cauliflower mixture in blender and purée until smooth and creamy. Combine this sauce with crabmeat, blending thoroughly. Spoon mixture into 2-quart casserole. Cover and bake at 350° for 30 minutes. Serve over hot cooked rice.

SERVINGS: 4

PER SERVING
Calories: 253
Fat: 1.7 grams
Cholesterol·   57 milligrams

Broiled Swordfish Steak

1	pound swordfish
¼	cup lemon juice
	Butter Buds equivalent to 3 tablespoons butter
½	teaspoon oregano
2	cloves garlic, finely minced
⅛	teaspoon salt
	Salt and pepper (optional)
2	tablespoons finely minced fresh parsley
1	lemon, cut into wedges

Wash swordfish and pat dry with paper towels. Place in broiler pan. Combine lemon juice, Butter Buds, oregano, garlic, and salt. Brush swordfish with lemon juice mixture and broil for 5 to 7 minutes on each side, basting several times while broiling. Remove fish from broiler and place on hot serving platter. Season with additional salt and pepper, if desired. Sprinkle with minced parsley and serve immediately with lemon wedges.

SERVINGS: **4**

PER SERVING
Calories·	110
Fat:	3.3 grams
Cholesterol:	50 milligrams

Honey-Glazed Scallops

3	tablespoons white wine
1	tablespoon soy sauce
¼	cup pineapple juice
½	teaspoon dry mustard
2	teaspoons honey
1	tablespoon brown sugar
1	pound scallops (bay or sea)

Combine white wine, soy sauce, pineapple juice, dry mustard, honey, and brown sugar. Marinate scallops in this mixture for about 1 hour. (Refrigerate while marinating.) Remove scallops from marinade, arrange on broiler pan, and broil for 7 to 10 minutes on each side, basting occasionally with marinade. (Adjust broiling time according to size of scallops.)

SERVINGS: 4

PER SERVING
Calories:	141
Fat:	1 gram
Cholesterol:	45 milligrams

Salmon in Herbs and Lemon

1	cup chopped scallions
4	lemons
1	pound salmon fillets or steaks
½	teaspoon oregano
⅛	teaspoon garlic powder
	Salt and pepper to taste

Place half of the scallions and the juice of 2 lemons on the bottom of a glass baking dish. Arrange salmon on top of scallions. Top with remaining scallions and the juice of the other 2 lemons. Season with oregano, garlic powder, salt, and pepper. Bake uncovered at 350° for 30 minutes, or until fish flakes. Baste with juices once or twice while baking.

SERVINGS: **4**

PER SERVING
Calories:	175
Fat:	4.8 grams
Cholesterol:	30 milligrams

Baked Salmon Steaks

4 scallions, chopped
4 tablespoons oil-free Italian salad dressing
2 medium salmon steaks (about ¾ pound)
Butter Buds equivalent to 2 tablespoons
butter
Salt and pepper to taste

Place half of the chopped scallions and half of the salad dressing on the bottom of a shallow baking dish. Arrange salmon on top of scallions and dressing. Top with remaining scallions and dressing, and the Butter Buds, salt, and pepper. Bake uncovered at 350° for 30 minutes, or until fish flakes.

SERVINGS: 2

PER SERVING
Calories: 218
Fat: 6.7 grams
Cholesterol: 45 milligrams

Stuffed Trout with Lemon Sauce

1 cup chopped onions
½ cup chopped green peppers
1½ cups coarse breadcrumbs from nonfat bread
Egg substitute equivalent to 1 egg
Butter Buds equivalent to 4 tablespoons butter
1 tablespoon chopped fresh parsley
¼ teaspoon garlic powder
½ teaspoon salt
¼ teaspoon pepper
4 medium brook trout, boned
Lemon sauce (¼ cup lemon juice mixed with Butter Buds flavoring equivalent to 2 tablespoons butter)

Dry-sauté onions and peppers in nonstick skillet until tender. Cool 2 to 3 minutes. Add breadcrumbs, egg substitute, Butter Buds, parsley, and seasonings; mix well. Stuff trout with filling and arrange in shallow baking dish. Drizzle lemon sauce over trout and bake uncovered at 350° for 30 to 35 minutes, or until fish flakes. Add more lemon juice, if necessary, to prevent sticking.

SERVINGS: 4

PER SERVING
Calories: 193
Fat: 2.2 grams
Cholesterol: 55 milligrams

Baked Haddock with Mushroom Stuffing

½ cup minced onions
1 4-ounce can mushrooms, finely chopped (reserve liquid)
1 clove garlic, minced
½ teaspoon oregano
Few sprigs fresh parsley, chopped
¼ teaspoon salt
Pepper to taste (optional)
1 cup whole-wheat breadcrumbs from nonfat bread
1 pound haddock
Butter Buds equivalent to 1 teaspoon butter
2 tablespoons lemon juice

Sauté onions, mushrooms, and garlic in small amount of reserved mushroom liquid until tender. Add oregano, parsley, salt, and pepper. Add breadcrumbs and toss until crumbs absorb moisture. (If a moister stuffing is desired, add more reserved mushroom liquid or a small amount of water.) Arrange haddock in a shallow baking dish and spoon stuffing evenly over top of fish. Combine Butter Buds and lemon juice and drizzle over fish and stuffing. Bake uncovered at 350° for 35 minutes, or until fish flakes.

SERVINGS: 4

PER SERVING			
Calories:	155	Fat:	0.5 gram
		Cholesterol:	68 milligrams

Broiled Marinated Snapper

> 1 pound red snapper fillets (or similar white-
> meat fish)
> ¼ cup oil-free Italian salad dressing
> 1 clove garlic, minced
> 1 tablespoon lemon juice
> 1 lemon, cut into wedges
> Salt and pepper (optional)

Marinate snapper in salad dressing, garlic, and lemon juice for several hours. Refrigerate while marinating. Remove fish from marinade and broil for about 5 minutes on each side, or until fish flakes. Baste with marinade while broiling. Serve with lemon wedges. Season with salt and pepper, if desired.

SERVINGS: 4

PER SERVING
Calories: 96
Fat: 0.9 gram
Cholesterol: 56 milligrams

Monkfish al Diavolo

1¼	pounds monkfish fillets
	Butter Buds equivalent to 1 tablespoon butter
¼	teaspoon salt
½	teaspoon oregano
1	tablespoon lemon juice
1	10-ounce can stewed tomatoes, chopped
1	teaspoon tomato paste
½	teaspoon crushed red pepper

Arrange monkfish on broiler pan. Sprinkle with Butter Buds, salt, oregano, and lemon juice. Broil fillets for about 5 minutes on each side, or until tender. Meanwhile combine stewed tomatoes, tomato paste, and crushed pepper in a small saucepan. Heat thoroughly. Spoon hot sauce over fish and serve immediately.

SERVINGS: 4

PER SERVING
Calories: 114
Fat: 1.1 grams
Cholesterol: 62 milligrams

POTATOES, RICE, BREADS, AND STUFFINGS

Whipped Potatoes

> 5 medium potatoes
> Butter Buds equivalent to 3 tablespoons butter
> ½ teaspoon salt (or to taste)
> 1 tablespoon onion powder
> ¾ cup skim milk

Peel and cube potatoes. Place in saucepan and cover with water. Bring to a boil and cook until tender (about 20 minutes). Drain potatoes and mash with a fork or ricer. Add seasonings and beat on high speed with an electric mixer, gradually adding milk to obtain desired consistency. Continue whipping on high speed until fluffy. Serve immediately.

SERVINGS: 4

PER SERVING
Calories: 136
Fat: 0.2 gram
Cholesterol: 1 milligram

Scalloped Potatoes Italiano

4	medium potatoes
1	tablespoon minced fresh parsley
½	teaspoon salt
⅛	teaspoon pepper
⅛	teaspoon garlic powder
½	cup nonfat plain yogurt
1	cup chopped onions
	Butter Buds equivalent to 2 tablespoons butter
	Skim milk (optional)

Peel potatoes and cut into thin slices. Beginning with potatoes, layer ingredients in a glass baking dish as follows: potatoes, seasonings, yogurt, and onions. Repeat the layers. Top with Butter Buds. Cover and bake at 350° for 1 hour, or until potatoes are cooked. If necessary, add a small amount of skim milk to prevent sticking.

SERVINGS: 4

PER SERVING
Calories:	126
Fat:	0.3 gram
Cholesterol:	1 milligram

Baked Potatoes Vesuvio

4 large baking potatoes
½ cup evaporated skim milk
½ cup nonfat plain yogurt
Salt and pepper to taste
Sprinkle of paprika

Bake potatoes at 350° until done (about 60 to 70 minutes); set aside to cool slightly. Cut thin slice off top of each potato. Scoop out potato pulp, leaving just enough to allow potato skins to retain their shape. Place potato pulp in medium mixing bowl and mash with fork. Add evaporated milk and yogurt; season with salt and pepper. Whip with electric mixer until smooth and creamy. Fill potato skins with whipped potatoes and sprinkle with paprika. Place in 400° oven for about 15 minutes, or until potatoes are lightly browned.

SERVINGS: 4

PER SERVING
Calories: 120
Fat: 0.2 gram
Cholesterol: 1.5 milligrams

Potatoes L'Arancia

4	medium potatoes, peeled and cubed
½	cup skim milk
¾	teaspoon salt
¼	teaspoon pepper
	Juice of 1 orange
1	tablespoon minced fresh parsley
	Grated rind of 1 orange

Boil the potatoes 20 minutes (until done) and mash them. Add milk, salt, pepper, and orange juice and beat well. Fold in minced parsley. Place potatoes in nonstick casserole and sprinkle with grated orange rind. Bake at 350° for 20 minutes. Serve hot.

SERVINGS: 4

PER SERVING
Calories: 120
Fat: 0.4 gram
Cholesterol: 0.5 milligram

Fried Potatoes

4 medium baking potatoes
Salt and pepper to taste
Onion powder to taste

Bake potatoes in 350° oven for about 45 minutes to 1 hour. Cool, preferably in refrigerator, for several hours. Remove skins and slice as French fries or steak fries, or as desired. Arrange on nonstick cookie sheet. Sprinkle with seasonings and "fry" in hot oven (425°) until brown (about 25 minutes), turning occasionally.

SERVINGS: 4

PER SERVING
Calories: 100
Fat: 0.2 gram
Cholesterol: none

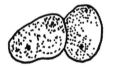

Mashed Sweet Potatoes

4 medium sweet potatoes
½ cup skim milk
Butter Buds equivalent to 2 tablespoons butter
1 teaspoon brown sugar

Scrub sweet potatoes, place in saucepan, and cover with water. Bring to a boil and cook until potatoes can be easily pierced with a fork (about 50 minutes). Remove from heat, drain, and cool slightly. Remove skins and mash with a fork. Add milk, Butter Buds, and brown sugar. Whip with an electric mixer until fluffy. Additional milk may be necessary if a thinner consistency is desired. (Potatoes may be reheated by placing them over water in the top section of a double boiler.)

SERVINGS: 4

PER SERVING
Calories: 168
Fat: 0.7 gram
Cholesterol: 0.5 milligram

Mashed Yams and Pineapple

3 medium yams (or sweet potatoes)
¼ cup crushed pineapple in juice
½ cup skim milk
¼ teaspoon cinnamon
1 teaspoon brown sugar

Wash yams. Place in saucepan, cover with water, and boil until well done (about 50 minutes). When yams are cool enough to handle, remove skins and mash well. Add all other ingredients and whip with electric mixer until smooth and creamy. (Place in top of double boiler, with water in bottom section, to reheat.)

SERVINGS: 4

PER SERVING
Calories: 140
Fat: 0.6 gram
Cholesterol: 0.5 milligram

Sicilian-Style Rice

1½	cups chopped green peppers
1	cup chopped onions
1	tablespoon red wine
1	cup crushed tomatoes
1	tablespoon tomato paste
½	teaspoon salt
¼	teaspoon pepper
2	cups cooked brown rice

Sauté green peppers and onions in wine. Combine tomatoes and tomato paste and add to peppers and onions. Season with salt and pepper. Cover and simmer until tender (about 15 minutes). Pour over hot cooked rice and mix thoroughly.

SERVINGS: 8

PER SERVING
Calories: 84
Fat: 0.2 gram
Cholesterol: none

Rice with Pineapple

1	cup brown rice
2¾	cups water
	Butter Buds equivalent to 2 tablespoons butter
⅓	cup chopped scallions
1	teaspoon soy sauce
1	cup crushed pineapple in juice

Boil rice in water and Butter Buds for 35 to 40 minutes, or until rice is tender. Dry-sauté scallions in large non-stick skillet until tender. Add soy sauce and pineapple and juice; mix well. Add cooked rice and toss until thoroughly blended. Simmer a few minutes, stirring constantly, until rice is hot.

SERVINGS: 8

PER SERVING
Calories: 100
Fat: 0.2 gram
Cholesterol: none

Brown Rice with Mushrooms

½	cup brown rice
1¼	cups water
1	teaspoon salt
¼	cup finely chopped onions
1	4-ounce can sliced mushrooms (reserve liquid)
3	tablespoons apple juice
	Butter Buds equivalent to 6 tablespoons butter
1	teaspoon lemon juice
2	tablespoons minced fresh parsley

Boil rice in water and salt until all water is absorbed and rice is tender (about 35 minutes). Rinse rice with cold water, drain, and set aside. In a nonstick skillet, sauté onions and mushrooms in apple juice until onions are tender. Add Butter Buds and cooked rice, blending thoroughly. Heat rice, stirring constantly. (Add small amount of reserved mushroom liquid, if necessary, to prevent sticking.) Sprinkle lemon juice over rice. Fold in minced parsley and heat 1 minute longer.

SERVINGS: 4

PER SERVING
Calories: 100
Fat: 0.3 gram
Cholesterol: none

Rice L'Arancio

½ cup minced onions
2 medium oranges
2 cups cooked rice
Butter Buds equivalent to 3 tablespoons butter
⅓ cup orange juice
10 seedless grapes, halved

Sauté onions until tender in large nonstick skillet with small amount of water to prevent sticking. Peel, seed, section, and chop oranges; add to skillet and stir over low heat for 1 or 2 minutes. Add cooked rice, Butter Buds, and orange juice. Toss until well mixed. Continue cooking, stirring constantly, until rice is thoroughly heated. If necessary, add additional orange juice to prevent sticking. Add grapes and toss just before removing from heat.

SERVINGS: 6

PER SERVING
Calories: 118
Fat: 0.3 gram
Cholesterol: none

Stromboli

1	1-pound ball of bread dough (page 136) or pizza dough made without shortening
½	cup chopped plum tomatoes, well drained
1½	cups chopped onions
3	ounces turkey pastrami, thinly sliced or shaved
2	teaspoons oregano
½	teaspoon garlic powder
	Salt and pepper to taste

Place risen dough on floured board. Flatten and stretch dough into rectangle approximately 12 × 15 inches. Spread ingredients over the surface of the dough in the following order: tomatoes, onions, pastrami, oregano, garlic powder, salt, and pepper. Roll dough lengthwise in jelly-roll fashion. Pinch edges to secure ingredients. (Roll will resemble loaf of French bread.) Carefully place roll on nonstick cookie sheet, and bake at 400° for about 40 minutes, or until golden brown. Cool well. Cut into ¾-inch slices just before serving.

SERVINGS: 18 slices

PER SERVING
Calories: 76
Fat: 0.4 gram
Cholesterol: 4 milligrams

No-Cheese, No-Oil Pizza

1	pound bread dough prepared with no shortening*
2	cups crushed tomatoes in purée
1	4-ounce can sliced mushrooms
½	cup chopped onions
½	cup shredded turkey pastrami
¼	cup chopped green peppers
1	teaspoon oregano
½	teaspoon garlic powder
	Salt and pepper to taste

Stretch risen dough out on large cookie sheet (approximately 15 × 10 inches). Spoon tomatoes over dough, distributing evenly. Distribute remaining ingredients evenly on top of tomatoes. Bake at 350° for about 40 minutes, or until crust is brown and crisp. Slice and serve.

SERVINGS: 12 slices

PER SERVING
Calories: 127
Fat: 1.1 grams
Cholesterol: 7 milligrams

*Frozen bread doughs usually contain shortening, but many local pizza houses make a dough without shortening, or one with just a minimal amount of vegetable oil. Italian Wheat Bread dough (next page) may also be used.

Italian Wheat Bread

1	package or cake yeast
1	cup warm water
½	teaspoon sugar
½	teaspoon salt
3½	cups whole-wheat flour

In a large bowl, combine the yeast and water; add the sugar and salt. Stir in about half of the flour and mix with a wooden spoon until smooth. Gradually add remaining flour to form a soft dough. Place on floured surface and knead until smooth and elastic (about 8 minutes). Place dough in pot with nonstick surface, cover, and let rise until dough doubles in size (about 1½ to 2 hours). Knead again for 1 to 2 minutes, cover, and let rise for another hour. Place dough on floured surface and roll into 8 × 18-inch rectangle. Starting with the wide side, roll dough tightly into a long cylinder. Pinch edges of dough to secure them. Place on nonstick cookie sheet. Cut slashes on top surface of loaf, about 2 inches apart. Using a pastry brush, brush surface of loaf with cold water and set aside to rise for another hour. Bake at 400° for 45 minutes, or until brown. Brush two or three times with cold water while baking.

SERVINGS: 24 ¾-inch slices

PER SERVING			
Calories:	58	Fat:	0.1 gram
		Cholesterol:	none

Italian Melba Toast

1 loaf nonfat Italian bread (previous page)
Salt to taste
Garlic powder to taste

Cut bread into ½-inch-thick slices and arrange on non-stick cookie sheet. Lightly season both sides with salt and garlic powder. Bake bread slices in 300° oven until dry, crisp, and light brown (about 50 minutes). Serve as you would Melba toast, with soups and salads, or as a snack with jelly or preserves. The slices may be cubed and used as croutons, as well.

SERVINGS: 36 slices

PER SERVING (1 slice)
Calories: 39
Fat: 0.1 gram
Cholesterol: none

Apple Bread Stuffing

2¾	cups water
1	chicken bouillon cube
	Butter Buds equivalent to ½ cup butter
1	cup chopped celery
1	cup chopped onions
4	cups whole-wheat breadcrumbs (made from nonfat bread such as pita bread)
	Salt and pepper to taste
½	teaspoon sage
2	cups diced apples

Boil water. Add bouillon cube, Butter Buds, celery, and onions. Simmer 5 minutes. Add breadcrumbs and toss until all liquid is absorbed. Season with salt, pepper, and sage. Add apples and mix thoroughly. (Additional water may be used if a moister stuffing is desired.) Spoon stuffing into a 2-quart nonstick casserole. Cover and bake at 350° for 45 minutes to 1 hour. Remove cover for final 10 to 15 minutes to brown lightly.

SERVINGS: 10

PER SERVING
Calories: 95
Fat: 0.1 gram
Cholesterol: none

Stuffing for Fish

<table>
<tr><td>1</td><td>cup finely chopped onions</td></tr>
<tr><td>1</td><td>cup red or green peppers</td></tr>
<tr><td></td><td>Butter Buds equivalent to ¼ cup butter</td></tr>
<tr><td>¼</td><td>cup fish stock or defatted chicken broth</td></tr>
<tr><td></td><td>Egg substitute equivalent to 1 egg</td></tr>
<tr><td>1½</td><td>cups coarse breadcrumbs from nonfat bread</td></tr>
<tr><td></td><td>Salt and pepper to taste</td></tr>
</table>

Dry-sauté onions and peppers in nonstick skillet. Add Butter Buds and stock. Remove from heat and cool slightly. Add egg substitute and breadcrumbs and toss until crumbs are well moistened. Add a little more water, if necessary. Season with salt and pepper to taste. Use as a stuffing for fish. Makes about 2 cups of stuffing.

SERVINGS: 8 (¼ cup each)

PER SERVING
Calories: 56
Fat: 0.1 gram
Cholesterol: none

DESSERTS
AND
FRUIT SALADS

Delicious Nonfattening Cheesecake

½ cup sugar
Egg substitute equivalent to 6 eggs
2 pounds low-fat cottage cheese (1% or less)
6 tablespoons flour
½ teaspoon baking powder
2 tablespoons grated lemon rind
1 teaspoon vanilla extract

Combine sugar and egg substitute and beat on medium speed with electric mixer for 1 minute. Add cottage cheese and continue to beat until smooth and creamy. Sift flour and baking powder together. Add gradually to cheese mixture, blending thoroughly after each addition. Add grated lemon rind and vanilla extract and beat for 1 minute. Pour into 10-inch springform pan. Bake at 350° for 1 hour, or until toothpick inserted into center of cake comes out clean. Let cool; remove rim of springform pan, place cheesecake on large plate, and refrigerate until well chilled.

SERVINGS: 12

PER SERVING
Calories: 95
Fat: 0.3 gram
Cholesterol: 4 milligrams

Strawberry and Cream Crêpes

Crêpes
   Egg substitute equivalent to 1 egg
½   cup flour
½   teaspoon sugar
½   cup skim milk

Filling
1   cup low-fat cottage cheese (1% or less)
3   tablespoons sugar
1   teaspoon vanilla extract
2   cups sliced strawberries

To make the crêpes, place egg substitute in medium bowl. Add flour and sugar, mixing well. Add milk gradually and beat with a whisk or electric beater until batter is smooth. Heat 7-inch crêpe pan or nonstick skillet. Pour in 2 to 3 tablespoons of batter, then lift pan above the heating unit and tilt in all directions, allowing batter to coat bottom of pan. (This must be done quickly, before batter sets.) Return pan to heating unit and cook on medium heat until lightly browned on bottom and dry on top. Carefully loosen edges of crêpe and flip it over. Cook on opposite side for about 20 seconds. Remove crêpe from pan and place on paper towels to cool. Repeat until all batter has been used up. Makes about 8 crêpes.

For the filling, combine cottage cheese, sugar, and vanilla and whip with electric mixer until smooth and creamy. Fold in strawberries. Place a crêpe on plate and spoon filling along center of crêpe. Fold one side of the crêpe over filling. Then fold over the other side, so that it overlaps the first. Fill remaining crêpes in same manner. Serve immediately or chill until ready to serve.

SERVINGS: 8

PER SERVING
Calories: 84
Fat: 0.4 gram
Cholesterol: 2 milligrams

Baked Apple-Pineapple Delight

6	medium apples, pared and sliced
1	teaspoon lemon juice
1	cup crushed pineapple in juice (undrained)
½	cup brown sugar
3	tablespoons cornstarch
¼	teaspoon cinnamon

Place sliced apples in bowl and toss with lemon juice. Arrange half of the apples in the bottom of a 9-inch-square baking dish. Spoon crushed pineapples and juice over apples; then top with remaining apples. Combine sugar, cornstarch, and cinnamon and sprinkle evenly over apples. Bake at 350° for 40 minutes. Serve warm or chilled.

SERVINGS: 8

PER SERVING
Calories: 127
Fat: 0.2 gram
Cholesterol: none

Strawberry-and-Cheese-Filled Meringues

Meringue
- 2 egg whites
- ¼ teaspoon vanilla extract
- ½ cup sugar (slightly less may be used, if desired)

Filling
- 1 cup low-fat cottage cheese (1% or less)
- 3 tablespoons sugar
- 1 teaspoon vanilla extract
- 2 cups sliced strawberries

- 8 whole strawberries

To make the meringue, beat egg whites and vanilla with electric mixer until soft peaks are formed. Gradually add sugar and continue beating until stiff peaks are formed. Divide meringue into 8 equal mounds on cookie sheet covered with unglazed brown paper (a paper bag is perfect). Using the back of a spoon, make a well or indentation in the center of each mound. Bake at 300° for 40 to 45 minutes, until shells are dry and lightly browned. Remove from oven and set aside to cool. Carefully remove from cookie sheet with spatula.

For the filling, combine cottage cheese, sugar, and vanilla and whip with electric mixer until smooth and creamy. Fold in sliced strawberries. Spoon mixture equally into the 8 cool meringue shells. Top each with a whole strawberry. Refrigerate until ready to serve.

SERVINGS: 8

PER SERVING
Calories: 95
Fat: 0.3 gram
Cholesterol: 1.5 milligrams

Crème Caramel

Egg substitute equivalent to 4 eggs
9 tablespoons sugar
1 teaspoon vanilla extract
4 cups warm skim milk
1 teaspoon lemon juice

In a medium mixing bowl, beat egg substitute, 4 table-spoons sugar, and vanilla on low speed with electric mixer. Gradually add warm milk, and continue beating on low speed until well blended. Set aside. Place remaining 5 tablespoons sugar and lemon juice in small saucepan over low heat. Cook, stirring constantly, until sugar begins to caramelize (becomes brown and foamy). Pour caramelized sugar into 1½-quart oven-proof mold or Bundt pan. (Individual custard cups may be used. If used, spoon equal amounts of caramelized sugar into each cup.) Rotate mold, or cups, to coat with sugar. Place mold, or cups, in large pan containing about 1 inch of hot water. Place in 325° oven and bake for about 45 minutes, or until toothpick inserted into center of mold comes out clean. (Individual custard cups may require less baking time.) Remove from oven and cool. Refrigerate until thoroughly chilled before serving.

SERVINGS: 8

PER SERVING
Calories: 113

Fat: 0.5 gram
Cholesterol: 2 milligrams

Chocolate Meringue Pie

Pie Shell
- 1   cup nonfat cornflake crumbs
- 3   tablespoons frozen apple juice concentrate, thawed and undiluted

Filling
- ½   cup sugar
- 2   tablespoons cornstarch
- 2   tablespoons cocoa powder
- ½   teaspoon salt
- 2   cups skim milk

Meringue
- 2   egg whites
- 2   tablespoons sugar

To make the pie shell, place cornflake crumbs in medium bowl and sprinkle with apple juice concentrate; blend with fork. Press crumbs into 9-inch pie plate, covering bottom and sides. Bake at 400° for 12 minutes, or until crust is brown. Remove from oven and set aside to cool.

To make the filling, combine the sugar, cornstarch, cocoa, and salt in a medium saucepan. Gradually stir in milk and cook over medium heat until mixture boils. Continue boiling for about 1 or 2 minutes, until mixture begins to thicken, stirring constantly. Remove from heat and cool for 5 minutes; then pour into baked piecrust. Set pie aside to cool and set.

To prepare the meringue, place egg whites in medium mixing bowl and beat with an electric mixer until frothy. Gradually add the sugar and continue beating on high speed until meringue forms stiff peaks. In a swirling fashion, spread meringue over pie, making certain to cover all the filling. Place pie into 400° oven for about 10 minutes, or until meringue is almost golden. Remove from oven and cool; then refrigerate until pie is thoroughly chilled.

SERVINGS: 10

PER SERVING
Calories: 110
Fat: 0.4 gram
Cholesterol: 1 milligram

Angel Food Cake

½	cup sifted flour
¾	cup sugar
⅛	teaspoon salt
6	egg whites
½	teaspoon vanilla extract
½	teaspoon cream of tartar

Combine flour, ¼ cup sugar, and salt; sift twice and set aside. With an electric mixer, beat egg whites, vanilla, and cream of tartar on high speed until soft peaks form. Add remaining sugar gradually and continue beating until stiff peaks form. Place flour mixture in sifter and sift flour gradually over egg whites, folding in after each addition. Repeat until all flour has been folded in. Pour into nonstick loaf pan. Bake at 375° for 25 to 30 minutes, or until toothpick inserted in center comes out clean. Invert cake, resting each end of loaf pan on a raised object, such as a book, in order that cake may cool in an upside-down position without touching the table. Loosen with spatula and remove cake from pan after it is thoroughly cool.

SERVINGS: 12

PER SERVING
Calories: 76
Fat: 0.1 gram
Cholesterol: none

Rice Pudding

⅓ cup uncooked brown rice
¼ cup water
2 cups skim milk
2 tablespoons sugar
⅛ teaspoon salt
Egg substitute equivalent to 1 egg
1 teaspoon vanilla extract
¼ cup raisins
Cinnamon to taste

Combine rice, water, 1½ cups skim milk, sugar, and salt in saucepan. Bring to a boil while stirring constantly. Reduce heat, cover, and simmer about 20 minutes, or until rice is tender. Combine remaining skim milk, egg substitute, and vanilla and beat slightly. Add to cooked rice and continue cooking over low heat until thick and creamy (about 12 more minutes). Fold in raisins. Spoon into dessert dishes and sprinkle with cinnamon. Chill.

SERVINGS: 4

PER SERVING
Calories: 153
Fat: 0.2 gram
Cholesterol: 2 milligrams

Strawberry Shortcake

1	¾-inch slice angel food cake (page 152)
½	cup sliced fresh strawberries
1	tablespoon whipped dessert topping (page 171)

Put slice of angel food cake on dessert plate. Top with fresh strawberries and whipped dessert topping.

SERVINGS: 1

PER SERVING
Calories: 120
Fat: 0.5 gram
Cholesterol: 1 milligram

Pudding and Peach Pie

Pie Shell
- 1 cup nonfat cornflake crumbs
- 1 tablespoon brown sugar
- 3 tablespoons frozen apple juice concentrate, thawed and undiluted

Filling
- ½ cup granulated sugar
- 2 tablespoons cornstarch
- ½ teaspoon salt
- 2 cups skim milk
- 1 teaspoon vanilla extract

- 2 fresh peaches, peeled and sliced

To make the crust, combine cornflake crumbs, brown sugar, and apple juice concentrate in a medium bowl; blend thoroughly with a fork. Press crumbs into 9-inch pie plate, covering bottom and sides. Bake at 400° for 10 to 12 minutes, or until crust is brown. Cool.

To make the filling, combine granulated sugar, cornstarch, and salt in a medium saucepan. Gradually stir in milk and cook over medium heat until mixture boils, stirring constantly. Add vanilla and continue cooking for another 1 to 2 minutes, until pudding thickens. Cool for 5 minutes, then pour into baked piecrust.

Chill pie until pudding sets; then arrange sliced

peaches over filling and refrigerate until thoroughly chilled.

SERVINGS: 10

PER SERVING
Calories: 116
Fat: 0.2 gram
Cholesterol: 1 milligram

Chocolate Banana Pudding

½ cup sugar
2 tablespoons cornstarch
2 tablespoons cocoa powder
½ teaspoon salt
2 cups skim milk
3 medium bananas (ripe)

In a medium saucepan, combine sugar, cornstarch, cocoa, and salt. Gradually stir in milk, and cook over medium heat until pudding boils and thickens, stirring constantly. Set aside to cool for about 5 minutes. Slice bananas and distribute evenly into 6 sherbet dishes. Pour pudding over bananas. Cool for additional 10 minutes; then chill in refrigerator until pudding is well set.

SERVINGS: 6

PER SERVING
Calories: 151
Fat: 0.8 gram
Cholesterol: 1 milligram

Baked Apple

1 medium apple
1 teaspoon brown sugar
1 teaspoon raisins
Sprinkle of cinnamon
Butter Buds equivalent to 1 teaspoon butter

Remove core from apple. Combine remaining ingredients and spoon mixture into center of cored apple. Place apple in small baking dish and bake uncovered for 30 minutes in 350° oven. If apple begins to stick to pan, add a small amount of water to bottom of pan and cover apple loosely with aluminum foil.

SERVINGS: 1

PER SERVING
Calories: 104
Fat: 0.1 gram
Cholesterol: none

Fresh Blueberries with Bananas

    1   pint fresh blueberries
    2   bananas
    1   tablespoon sugar
    1   tablespoon water
  ⅛   teaspoon grated lemon rind

Wash and drain blueberries; place in bowl. Slice bananas into bowl with blueberries. Sprinkle fruit with sugar, water, and lemon rind. Toss gently and serve in sherbet dishes.

SERVINGS: 6

PER SERVING
Calories: 82
Fat: 0.4 gram
Cholesterol: none

Fresh Pineapple with Strawberries

1 ripe fresh pineapple
1 pint fresh strawberries
1 tablespoon sugar (optional)

Remove skin and slice pineapple. Remove center core of each slice and discard. Cut pineapple slices into bite-size chunks. Wash, hull, and slice strawberries. Combine pineapple chunks and strawberries; add sugar and toss gently. Serve in sherbet dishes.

SERVINGS: 8

PER SERVING
Calories: 57
Fat: 0.3 gram
Cholesterol: none

Fresh Strawberries Limone

1	pint fresh strawberries
1	tablespoon sugar
1	tablespoon lemon juice
½	teaspoon grated lemon rind

Wash and hull strawberries; cut into halves. Toss gently with sugar, lemon juice, and grated lemon rind. Chill and serve in sherbet dishes.

SERVINGS: 4

PER SERVING
Calories: 40
Fat: 0.3 gram
Cholesterol: none

Summer Fruit and Cheese Plate

Outer leaves from head of lettuce
1 wedge watermelon (approximately 4 × 4 inches)
½ cantaloupe
1 slice fresh pineapple, ½ inch thick (core removed)
½ cup dry-curd cottage cheese
4 large fresh strawberries
10 red seedless grapes

Line dinner plate with lettuce leaves. Remove rind from watermelon and slice into smaller wedges. Slice cantaloupe into wedges and remove skin. Place pineapple slice in center of lettuce bed and top with cottage cheese. Arrange watermelon, cantaloupe, strawberries, and grapes attractively around pineapple and cheese. Serve well chilled.

SERVINGS: 1

PER SERVING
Calories: 256
Fat: 1.6 grams
Cholesterol: 6 milligrams

Fruit Kabobs

    2 cups watermelon balls
    2 cups cantaloupe balls
    2 cups honeydew melon balls
    1 pint large strawberries, washed and hulled
    1 cup fresh pineapple chunks

Use a fruit scoop to make the fruit balls. Then arrange fruit in alternating fashion on small wooden skewers.

SERVINGS: 6

PER SERVING
Calories: 88
Fat: 0.8 gram
Cholesterol: none

Strawberry Milkshake

          2   cups strawberries, hulled
          ½   ripe banana
        1½   cups skim milk
          ½   cup nonfat plain yogurt
                Sugar substitute (optional)

Place strawberries and banana in blender and purée. Add milk and yogurt and blend again until creamy and frothy. Pour into chilled glasses. Add a small amount of sugar substitute while blending if a sweeter taste is desired.

SERVINGS: 4

PER SERVING
Calories: 93
Fat: 0.9 gram
Cholesterol: 2 milligrams

Pineapple-Orange Cooler

1½ to 2   cups crushed ice
     1   cup crushed pineapple in juice
     1   cup orange juice
     4   tablespoons nonfat dry milk powder
   ¼   cup water

Place 1 cup crushed ice and all other ingredients in a blender and blend on high speed until smooth and frothy. Add remaining ice and blend for 20 seconds, or until thick and creamy.

SERVINGS: **4**

PER SERVING
Calories: 76
Fat: 0.1 gram
Cholesterol: 1 milligram

TOPPINGS
AND
SAUCES

Low-Fat Sour Cream

> ¼ cup nonfat plain yogurt
> 1 cup low-fat cottage cheese (1% or less)
> 1 tablespoon vinegar

Place ingredients in blender and blend until smooth and creamy. Chill. Use as a topping for baked potatoes, as a vegetable enhancer, or in recipes that call for sour cream. Makes a little over 1 cup.

SERVINGS: 16
PER SERVING   (1 generous tablespoon)
Calories: 9
Fat: 0.1 gram
Cholesterol: 1 milligram

Fruit Salad Topping

> ½ cup nonfat plain yogurt
> ¾ cup fresh strawberries, washed and hulled
> ⅛ teaspoon vanilla extract

Combine all ingredients in blender and purée until strawberries are well blended and mixture is smooth and creamy. Chill before serving as a fruit salad topping. Makes about 1 cup.

Variation: Substitute ¾ cup crushed pineapple in juice (drained) for strawberries.

SERVINGS: 16

PER SERVING (1 tablespoon)
Calories: 7
Fat: 0.1 gram
Cholesterol: 0.5 milligram

Whipped Dessert Topping

½ cup low-fat cottage cheese (1% or less)
2 teaspoons powdered sugar
½ teaspoon vanilla extract
1 tablespoon skim milk

Combine all ingredients in blender or food processor and whip until smooth and creamy. Serve over fresh fruit, gelatin, or pudding. Makes about ½ cup.

SERVINGS: 8

PER SERVING (1 tablespoon)
Calories: 14
Fat: 0.1 gram
Cholesterol: 1 milligram

Seafood Cocktail Sauce

> ¼ cup tomato catsup
> 1 tablespoon prepared horseradish
> 1 tablespoon lemon juice
> Dash of Tabasco sauce (optional)

Combine all ingredients and chill well. Serve with broiled or grilled fish to enhance flavor.

SERVINGS: **5**

PER SERVING (1 tablespoon)
Calories: 15
Fat: 0.1 gram
Cholesterol: none

Hot Salsa Italian Style

1 cup canned crushed tomatoes
½ cup finely chopped green peppers
½ cup finely chopped onions
½ teaspoon crushed red pepper (adjust to taste)
 Salt to taste

Combine all ingredients and chill. Serve as a side dish to spice up cooked fish, poultry, or rice. Makes about 1½ cups.

SERVINGS: approximately 10
PER SERVING (2 generous tablespoons)
Calories: 10
Fat: none
Cholesterol: none

SUGGESTED MENUS

Below are a few of my family's favorite "go-togethers." If you have hearty appetites, and if your caloric and fat allowance permits it, you may wish to add an appetizer, a cup of soup, a pasta side dish, or a dessert from my recipe collection to your meal. Serving portions should be adjusted to meet your personal dietary needs.

Hunter's-Style Chicken Rosemary
Stuffed Mushrooms
Snow Peas L'Arancio
Tomato, Onion, and Cucumber Salad

Salmon in Herbs and Lemon
Rice with Pineapple
Sautéed Mushrooms
Lettuce with Oil-Free Dressing

Turkey Meatloaf (with onions and carrots)
Whipped Potatoes
Roasted Mushrooms

Chicken Rollatini in Tomato Sauce
Sicilian-Style Rice
Italian-Style Coleslaw

Cod Véronique
Scalloped Potatoes Italiano
Fried Cabbage and Apple Medley
Three-Bean Salad

Chicken Piccata
Mashed Yams and Pineapple
Glazed Cauliflower and Carrots
Waldorf Salad

Stuffed Trout with Lemon Sauce
Baked Potatoes Vesuvio
Breaded Artichoke Hearts
Orange Salad Roman Style

Monkfish al Diavolo
Stuffed Artichokes
Broccoli Italiano
Roasted Peppers

Grilled Lemon Chicken Breasts
Mashed Sweet Potatoes
Snow Peas L'Arancio
Lettuce with Oil-Free Dressing

Crabmeat Casserole
Brown Rice
Green Bean and Water Chestnut Salad

Roast Chicken with Herbs
Mock Eggplant Parmesan
Fresh Spinach and Mushroom Salad

Stuffed Turkey Bracciola
Brown Rice with Mushrooms
Baked Stuffed Acorn Squash
Hearts of Lettuce with Oil-Free Dressing

Melon with Pastrami Appetizer
Baked Ziti Ragu*
String Bean and Onion Salad

*Any pasta dish may be substituted here. Being a pasta lover, I serve a variation of this combination at least twice a week, with a different pasta each time.

TREAT YOUR GUESTS TO A LOW-FAT PARTY

Show off your new way of preparing foods by inviting your friends to a "Be Kind to Your Heart" party. In many cases, you'll be doing them a big favor. Your party can serve a dual purpose. First, you can put to rest the myth that a low-fat diet means sacrificing all goodies. Second, you will be able to share some of your recipes so that when your friends reciprocate the social invitation, you will find some familiar low-fat treats on their party tables. Who knows, you may start a new trend—a healthy one, to be sure!

Below is a suggested menu for a party of eight to ten guests. If you want to turn your party into a hearty buffet supper, add a salad or two and arrange a party tray with appropriate poultry cold cuts such as smoked turkey breast, turkey ham, and chicken breast.

1. Stromboli (single recipe)
2. No-Cheese, No-Oil Pizza (single recipe cut into party-size pieces)
3. Stuffed Mushrooms (double recipe)
4. Pepper and Onion Frittata (double recipe cut into bite-size quiche-like pieces)
5. Breaded Artichoke Hearts (double recipe)
6. Melon with Pastrami Appetizer (single recipe—cut melon into bite-size chunks, wrap with pastrami and pierce with party pick)

7. Monkfish Cocktail (double recipe)
8. Raw Vegetable Antipasto with Dip (single recipe)
9. Chickpea Nuts (double recipe)
10. Onion Dip with Italian Melba Toast (single recipe)
11. Fruit Kabobs (one per guest)

Have plenty of whole-wheat pita bread on hand.

INDEX